# THE
# SURRENDER OF
# SINGAPORE

# AUTHOR'S BIOGRAPHY

Stephen is a happily retired police officer having served with Essex Police as a constable for thirty years between 1983 and 2013. He is married to Tanya who is also his best friend.

His two sons, Luke and Ross, were members of the armed forces, collectively serving five tours in Afghanistan between 2008 and 2013. Both of them were injured on their first tours which led to the publication of Stephen's first book, *Two Sons in a Warzone – Afghanistan: The True Story of a Father's Conflict*, which was published in October 2010.

Stephen co-wrote a book published in August 2012 entitled *German POW Camp 266 – Langdon Hills*. It spent six weeks as the number one best-selling book in Waterstones, Basildon between March and April 2013.

Stephen has also co-written three crime thrillers, published between 2010 and 2012, which centre around a fictional detective named Terry Danvers.

He has also written numerous other books for Pen & Sword Books Limited, many of which were part of the Towns and Cities collection, which commemorated the sacrifices made by young men up and down the country during the First World War.

Both of Stephen's grandfathers served in and survived the First World War, one with the Royal Irish Rifles, the other in the Mercantile Navy, while his father was a member of the Royal Army Ordinance Corp during the Second World War.

When he is not writing, he and Tanya enjoy the simplicity of walking their dogs early each morning when most sensible people are still asleep.

# THE SURRENDER OF SINGAPORE

## Three Years of Hell 1942–45

### By Stephen Wynn

Pen & Sword
**MILITARY**

First published in Great Britain in 2017 by
**PEN & SWORD MILITARY**
an imprint of
Pen & Sword Books Ltd
47 Church Street
Barnsley
South Yorkshire
S70 2AS

ISBN 978-1-47382-402-7

A CIP catalogue record for this book is available from the British Library.

Printed and bound in England By
CPI Group (UK) Ltd, Croydon, CR0 4YY.

Pen & Sword Books Ltd incorporates the Imprints of Pen & Sword Aviation,
Pen & Sword Family History, Pen & Sword Maritime, Pen & Sword Military,
Pen & Sword Discovery, Pen & Sword Politics, Pen & Sword Atlas, Pen & Sword
Archaeology, Wharncliffe Local History, Wharncliffe True Crime, Wharncliffe
Transport, Pen & Sword Select, Pen & Sword Military Classics, Leo Cooper, The
Praetorian Press, Claymore Press, Remember When, Seaforth Publishing and
Frontline Publishing.

For a complete list of Pen & Sword titles please contact
PEN & SWORD BOOKS LIMITED
47 Church Street, Barnsley, South Yorkshire, S70 2AS, England
E-mail: enquiries@pen-and-sword.co.uk
Website: www.pen-and-sword.co.uk

# CONTENTS

# ACKNOWLEDGEMENTS

My thanks go out to Mrs Wynn Robertson for providing photographs of the MV *Krait* which can be found at the Australian Maritime Museum at Darling Harbour in Sydney. Also for the information which she provided in relation to the secret Second World War training camp, which was situated at Broken Bay, New South Wales.

My thanks also go to Mr Aron Manzanillo for providing photographs of the Civilian War Memorial which is situated within the War Memorial Park in Beach Road, immediately opposite the Swissotel at the Raffles City Shopping Mall in Singapore City. The memorial was built in memory of the local civilians who were killed during the Japanese occupation of Singapore during the Second World War. It was officially unveiled on 15 February 1967 by the then Prime Minister of Singapore, Mr Lee Kuan Yew.

# DEDICATION

This book is dedicated to the memories of all of the military personnel, nurses and civilians who were either killed during the Battle of Singapore in February 1942 or who died as a result of illness, disease, mistreatment or murder during the three and a half years of the Japanese occupation of the island from 15 February 1942 until 4 September 1945.

# PROLOGUE

What history has recorded as the Second World War took place in two separate locations. First there was the war that took place throughout Europe and North Africa and then there was the war in the Pacific and the Far East.

In Europe and North Africa, Britain and her allies were fighting against Nazi Germany and a dictator who wanted to rule Europe for a thousand years and beyond with an Aryan super race.

During the war the Nazis also embarked on a systematic extermination of Jewish people who lived in the nations that they conquered, stealing their properties and belongings as they went. They amassed fortunes from seized paintings, statues and other art works. They emptied churches and other religious sites of centuries-old works and anything else of any value. They stole cash and gold from banks and financial institutions for their own personal gain wherever they went.

Not happy with using extermination units to murder the Jews, they embarked on building a number of massive extermination camps to continue the killings on an industrial scale.

Then there was Japan, whose Imperial Army and Navy had decided that they wanted to rule the entire Pacific region as well as Far East Asia, and they even had half an eye on Australia as well.

The similarities between Germany and Japan can be traced back to the years between the First and Second World Wars, when they began their individual quests for domination and supremacy.

In Japan's case this went back even further. On 18 January 1915 she presented China with a list of twenty-one demands which, if adhered to, would have given Japan major control over most aspects of Chinese society and life.

On 19 September 1931 the Kwantung Army of the Empire of Japan invaded Manchuria, set up a puppet state, and stayed until the end of the Second World War. What was even more shocking was that the Kwantung Army had acted of their own volition and not with the support or say-so of the Japanese Government.

On 24 February 1933, Japan withdrew from the League of Nations in Geneva, after the assembly had adopted a report voted on by a majority of 42 to 1 which said Japan should withdraw her troops from Manchuria and restore the country to Chinese sovereignty. It was not a decision which went down well with the Japanese delegation.

The Second Sino-Japanese War began on 7 July 1937 and was fought between the Republic of China and the Empire of Japan, despite the latter's claims that all she wanted was peace throughout the Far East. In essence the war was the result of a long-standing Japanese imperialist policy that was aimed at securing access to economic resources, mainly in relation to food and labour, as well as the available raw materials that China had to offer.

The war in the Pacific and the Far East started on 7 December 1941 with the attack on the American Fleet at Pearl Harbor and the invasions in Hong Kong and Thailand. So much for Japan being a friendly and tranquil nation who only wanted peace in the region.

The next four years would be recorded historically and remembered by the world as a time of Japanese brutality and atrocities. A nation who had decided on a path of waging an aggressive war, in a world where as far as she was concerned there was no such thing as the Geneva Convention on Human Rights, the only rules were what she decided they would be. Some of her soldiers maltreated and murdered both foreign soldiers and civilians with equal disregard and appeared to place no value on human life whatsoever. They certainly did not act in the honourable way that the code of Bushido stated that they should. They showed little in the way of moral righteousness, courage, benevolence, respect, honesty, honour or loyalty to those that they captured and interned.

Yet again Britain and the rest of the Allied nations stood firm against a country who had determined that they were going to take control of the entire region for no other reason than they wanted to. Anyone who stood in their way would not be tolerated, and neither would anybody who they perceived to be anti-Japanese in their attitudes, actions or beliefs.

Britain and the Allied nations would prevail. They prevented a fanatical and tyrannical nation from waging aggressive warfare to enforce its own will over neighbouring countries.

In standing up against Germany and Japan, and preventing them from achieving their stated aims, all of the Allied nations paid a heavy price, with thousands of their own military personnel, as well as many more innocent civilians, being killed.

# CHAPTER ONE

# A BRIEF HISTORY OF SINGAPORE

Singapore today is a major centre for trade and commerce, a holiday destination, and a natural stop-off point for people travelling between Australasia and Europe.

Although Singapore has a history dating back to the third century, its modern history began in 1819 when Sir Stamford Raffles established a port on the island which helped it rapidly grow into a major trade route through South East Asia.

Starting in the sixteenth century large parts of South East Asia became colonised by some of the more affluent European countries such as Holland, Portugal and, to a lesser extent, Britain.

In 1818 Raffles became the Lieutenant Governor of the British held colony of Bencoolen on the island of Sumatra and became determined that Britain would replace the Dutch as the dominant power in the region. The saying that 'necessity is the mother of all invention' readily comes to mind, as it was because of the tactics employed by the Dutch in preventing British ships from either stopping at Dutch controlled ports or by charging them excessively high tax tariffs to do so that Raffles went off in search of a new location where a port could be built which would allow British ships to sail to and from China as well as what was then British India.

Raffles landed in Singapore on 28 January 1819 and quickly realized that this was exactly the type of location he was looking for. The island had a fresh water supply, enough trees whose timber could be used for the repairing of ships, as well as a deep enough water estuary which would allow for trading ships easily to stop there.

After some political gamesmanship on Raffles' part he acquired himself a formal treaty to establish a British trading post on the island, which was signed on 6 February 1919.

When Raffles first arrived in Singapore, the island had a population of about 1,000, mostly Malays and Chinese. Within the space of just fifty years that number had grown to over 100,000. Immigrant workers poured into Singapore from all over Asia to work in the newly established rubber plantations and tin mines.

One of the first decisions that Raffles made was to make the port of Singapore 'free', which meant that ships stopping there would not have to pay a tax levy on goods that they were either picking up or dropping off. Not surprisingly this quickly drew a lot of attention amongst traders who had previously had to pay taxes when entering a Dutch port in the region, so instead they now came pouring into Singapore free of charge.

Raffles left the island in what he thought were the capable hands of Major William Farquhar, along with a regiment of Indian soldiers and a few artillery pieces, and returned to Bencoolen. It would be three years before Raffles returned to Singapore and he wasn't totally happy with what he found on his return, so he replaced Farquhar with John Crawfurd, who was a physician, a diplomat and a colonial administrator. As the Governor of the island, he signed a new treaty with the island's leaders, on 7 June 1823, which in effect gave Britain complete administrative control and brought the island under British law.

Raffles left Singapore in October 1823 for what would be the final time and returned to England. He died there in 1826 at the age of 44.

The next one hundred years would see many changes taking place in Singapore. Those in charge would have to deal with many varied social issues, from protecting Chinese women who were forced into prostitution, to dealing with poor health and living standards and an acute housing shortage which got worse as more and more workers made their way to Singapore looking for work and a better life for themselves and their families.

Singapore didn't really have a part to play in the First World War as it was mainly a European conflict. The only thing of any real note which happened during that period was the 1915 mutiny by British Muslim Indian sepoys who were soldiers with the 5th Native Light Infantry and who were garrisoned in Singapore. Rumours started to spread amongst their ranks that they were soon to be sent to fight against the Ottoman Empire (today's Turkey) at Gallipoli. The Indian soldiers did not like the sound of that one bit, so they revolted, killing all of their officers as well as several civilians. The mutiny began on 15 February (the same day the Japanese occupied Singapore in 1942) and went on for several days before British, French, Russian and Japanese forces helped put down the rebellion. Forty-seven British soldiers and civilians lost their lives during seven days of mutiny.

A court of enquiry was quickly put in place on 23 February 1915, the day after the mutiny had been put down. A total of 200 of the sepoys were tried by court martial, 47 of whom were subsequently executed by firing squad at Outram Prison, a scene which was witnessed by an estimated crowd of some 15,000 people. The executions were carried out by men of the King's Shropshire Light Infantry and the Singapore Volunteer Corps. Another 73 of those found guilty received prison sentences ranging from 7 to 20 years.

On 15 February 1942, during the Second World War, Singapore came under the control of the Imperial Japanese Army, and would remain so for the next three and a half painful years.

After the war the island's economy would take several years to reach the levels it had been at prior to the Second World War, and it did so thanks to world demand for tin and rubber. In the eyes of most Singaporeans, Britain as a colonial leader, having failed to defend the island against the Japanese invasion, had lost all credibility. This directly led to an increase in nationalistic and anti-colonial fervour, eventually leading to Singapore gaining full independence on 9 August 1965. It had been a long journey, not without the odd hiccup along the way, including an amalgamation with Malaya to become Malaysia on 16 September 1963.

The country's first Prime Minister was Lee Kuan Yew who held the position for 31 years between 3 June 1959 and 28 November 1990.

# CHAPTER TWO

# SINGAPORE NAVAL BASE

Before the Second World War the naval base on Singapore had been something of a political hot potato for a number of years, with opinion divided on whether to strengthen the base or simply leave it well alone. As was the case with such matters, politics played a big part as to what did and did not happen. The following points are taken from the minutes of British Cabinet and British War Cabinet meetings.

At a War Cabinet meeting which took place on 3 October 1940, and which was chaired by the Prime Minister the Right Honourable Winston S Churchill, there were three items on the agenda for discussion which involved the Far East, not all of which were about Singapore, but they still had a relevance to the situation in the region.

Point five on the agenda was a discussion about the Burma Road Agreement and it was highlighted that the question wasn't really about whether Britain should reopen the Burma Road, more a question about when it should be done. The concern in the room appeared to be how to achieve this without announcing it in such a manner that it might appear provocative to the Japanese. The minutes of the meeting went on to say that the Prime Minister agreed that this was the right decision and that he did not believe that the Japanese would declare war upon Britain as a result.

Point six on the same agenda was a discussion about the general attitude of Japan. The Dutch Foreign Minister did not think that the Japanese were in a position to embark on any important new military adventures. Remember, if you will, this was two months away from the systematic planned attacks by Japan at Pearl Harbor, Hong Kong, Malaya, the Philippines and Thailand. How wrong was it possible for somebody to be?

There also appeared to be some doubt as to Britain's support of America in relation to her future involvement in a war with Japan. The Secretary of State for Foreign Affairs, The Right Honourable Viscount Halifax, clarified the matter, categorically stating that if the United States were at war with Japan, then Britain would declare war on her as well.

The suggestion had been made that a visit by the United States Naval Force to the naval base at Singapore would be viewed as a positive step.

Ten years earlier, on Wednesday, 28 May 1930, at a Cabinet meeting held at number ten Downing Street, the fourth item on that day's agenda was entitled 'The Singapore Base',

> *the conclusion of which was that the present slowed down programme should be allowed to continue and that arrangements should be made to obtain at the forthcoming Imperial Conference a definite and permanent settlement of the question of the Singapore Base.*
>
> *The Cabinet were reminded that it would be necessary to pay back to the Dominions and Colonies concerned any quota of their contributions towards the cost of the Singapore Base that might be received between the present time and the Imperial Conference.*

The Singapore Naval Base is situated at the northern tip of the island of Singapore and was both a British Royal Navy shore establishment and a major part of Britain's Far East defence policy between the First and Second World Wars.

With the clear rise in the military ambitions of the Japanese Empire throughout the Far East at the end of the First World War, the British Government decided that it made sound military sense to make available sufficient funds to begin building a naval base in Singapore. Not only did such an investment help safeguard Britain's own interests in the region but the hope was that it would also act as a visible deterrent to the Japanese.

The build was first announced in 1923, but at first it did not proceed with any apparent urgency – that was until the Japanese invasion of Manchuria in 1931. The naval base was finally completed in 1939 at a cost of some £60 million pounds. An equivalent cost today would be in excess of £3 billion pounds, a really staggering sum of money.

The new dock covered an area of twenty-one square miles and provided what was then the largest dry dock facility anywhere in the world. It had a floating dock and sufficient fuel tanks comfortably to support the entire British Navy for up to six months. It was a formidable structure and its defence was well supported by heavy fifteen-inch naval guns which were stationed at the nearby batteries at Johore, Changi, and Buona Vista. These in turn were supported by smaller batteries at Forts Siloso, Canning and Labrador, while the air defences for the base came from the nearby Royal Air Force bases at Tengah and Sembawang.

# CHAPTER THREE

# HMS *PRINCE OF WALES* – HMS *REPULSE*

HMS *Prince of Wales* was a battleship of the Royal Navy, a King George V class. It had been commissioned for service on 19 January 1941 out of the Cammell Laird shipyards in Birkenhead on the Wirral, Merseyside.

Although the *Prince of Wales* had a short service life, she had an interesting and varied one. On 22 May 1942, along with the battlecruiser *Hood* and six destroyers, she was ordered to the Atlantic, just south of Iceland, her intended target being the German Battleship *Bismarck*.

The *Bismarck* was spotted the very next day in company with the German heavy cruiser *Prinz Eugen* heading south westward in the area known as the Denmark Strait. Vice Admiral Lancelot Holland, who was on board HMS *Hood*, had ordered HMS *Prince of Wales*, HMS *Repulse*, six destroyers, and the cruisers *Norfolk* and *Suffolk* to make twenty-seven knots. Holland's plan was for his flagship, the *Hood*, along with the *Prince of Wales*, to concentrate on attacking the *Bismarck* while *Norfolk* and *Suffolk* were to concentrate on the *Prinz Eugen*. A potential problem for the *Hood* was that by now she was already twenty-five years old and it was questionable if her defensive armour was adequate for the type of enemy ships she would now be up against, even though she had undergone a major overhaul in March 1941. Accordingly, one of the tactics which she needed to employ was to get in close to prevent her being vulnerable to plunging enemy shellfire – which in turn potentially made her more vulnerable.

In the hours of darkness, and in what can only be described as inclement weather, with high seas, being engaged in a naval battle was not that straightforward an exercise. *Hood*, in all the confusion, actually opened up on the *Prinz Eugen* rather than the *Bismarck*, and the *Suffolk* and *Norfolk* were unclear as to what their roles were in the attack.

The battle commenced just before six o'clock in the morning, with the *Prinz Eugen* quickly striking the *Hood* with her eight-inch shells. The first salvo from the *Prince of Wales* was way off the mark, but two of her salvos finally struck the *Bismarck*, one striking her bow and the other entering her side armour belt and exploding, damaging the ship's boilers so extensively that she would have to return to port.

The *Hood* was sunk in the contact, having been struck by both the *Bismarck* and the *Prinz Eugen*. At the time of her sinking the *Hood* was the biggest battlecruiser in the world. Only three of her crew survived, the other 1,419 going to a watery grave.

The *Prince of Wales* was struck by two shells: one hit her on her starboard side and exploded; the second also struck her on the starboard side, and not only did it fail to go off but it wasn't even discovered until the *Prince of Wales* had returned to Rosyth in Scotland for repairs.

On 9 August 1941 the Prime Minister Winston Churchill, on board HMS *Prince of Wales*, arrived in Placentia Bay, Newfoundland, where he had a secret meeting with the American President, Franklin D. Roosevelt, to agree what was to be entitled the Atlantic Charter and which in essence set out the Allied goals for a new world order after the war.

Keeping up her busy schedule, after having returned to Scapa Flow from her American jaunt, she was soon off again, this time as part of an eighteen-ship convoy to Malta, leaving on 24 September 1941 and arriving back at Scapa Flow on 6 October.

She left for Singapore on 25 October 1941, finally arriving there on 2 December and becoming the flagship of Force Z, which was a British naval detachment whose main purpose was to reinforce British and Commonwealth assets in the Far East while at the same time deterring the Japanese expansion into British held colonies and assets, with particular attention to Malaya and Singapore. This was seen in some quarters as more of a political decision rather than a naval requirement.

On 10 December 1941 HMS *Prince of Wales*, along with HMS *Repulse*, left Singapore on route to investigate reports of Japanese troop landings at Kuantan, Thailand, which turned out to be false. The substance of the reports is not known but the resulting outcome was that both the *Prince of Wales* and the *Repulse* were caught in open sea without any kind of air cover at all. They were sitting ducks for Japanese aircraft to pick them off at will. It most certainly could have been a trap set by the Japanese to lure the British ships into the area so that they could attack them.

At eleven o'clock in the morning, the *Prince of Wales* was attacked by six torpedo-carrying Japanese aircraft. Half an hour into the attack the *Prince of Wales* was struck by a torpedo on the port side propeller shaft, causing her to list heavily. Then she was hit by a further four torpedoes and sunk. She lost 327 of her crew in the attack, including Vice Admiral Tom Phillips and Captain John Leach.

HMS *Repulse* was a Renown-class battlecruiser. At twenty-five years old, she was somewhat of an aging ship, having first been commissioned on 18 August 1916, during the First World War. She had two major refits, first in the 1920s and then again in the 1930s, which greatly increased her armour protection. She had accompanied HMS *Hood* on her round-the-world cruise of 1923-24 as well as helping to protect international shipping during the Spanish Civil War, 1936-39. During April to June 1940 she was involved in the Norwegian campaign. She was then involved in the hunt for the German battleship *Bismarck* from August to October 1941, before arriving in Singapore as part of Force Z in November 1941. She was destroyed during the same exchange which saw the demise of the *Prince of Wales*.

The Japanese submarine, the *I-58*, had first spotted Force Z at twenty past two on the morning of 10 December and fired a total of five torpedoes, but remarkably every single one of them missed their target.

HMS *Repulse* put up a remarkable fight, due in no small part to the maritime skills of her Captain, Bill Tennant. His anti-aircraft gunners damaged five of the attacking Japanese bombers while he managed to avoid being hit by a total of nineteen torpedoes. In the end it took a coordinated attack by seventeen Japanese Mitsubishi G4M torpedo bombers to finish off the *Repulse* who was eventually struck by five torpedoes. Before she was sunk, her gunners damaged a further eight Japanese aircraft as well as shooting down another two.

The *Repulse* lost a total of 508 officers and men and her survivors, who numbered nearly 1,000, were picked up by HMS *Electra* and HMS *Vampire*.

CHAPTER FOUR

# PARIT SULONG MASSACRE

The Parit Sulong Massacre took place on 23 January 1942, when an estimated 150 wounded soldiers from the Australian 8th Division and the 45th Indian Infantry Brigade, who had surrendered and been taken prisoner, were murdered by their Japanese captives. Those responsible were soldiers of the Imperial Guards Division of the Imperial Japanese Army.

During the Battle of Muar, which was the last major battle of the Malaya campaign, and which took place between 14 and 22 January 1942, Australian forces from 'B' Company, 2nd/30th Battalion, 8th Division, Australian Army, and who were under the command of Lieutenant Colonel Frederick Galleghan, became involved in a battle after they set an ambush that killed an estimated 1,000 Japanese soldiers. The Australians blew up the bridge that spanned the Kelamah River, and which connected the towns of Gemas and Tampin. Of the Japanese casualties, 700 of them were killed when the bridge was blown up. At the time of the ambush the Japanese were making their way to Gemas. The ensuing battle lasted for two days and resulted in the Australians having to eventually withdraw from Gemas and head south as quickly as they could.

On 20 January 1942, and just six days after the Australians had ambushed the Japanese at Gemas bridge, elements of the 2nd/19th Battalion, 8th Division, Australian Army, and about 1,000 Indian troops from the 45th Brigade, were situated in and around the town of Bakri which is only about five kilometres east of Muar. Lieutenant Colonel Charles Anderson, who was in command of all and any Commonwealth soldiers in the immediate area of Bakri, was ordered to pull out of the town and make his way to Yong Peng.

It was not to be an easy journey as their route was repeatedly halted by Japanese roadblocks, which meant more fighting and more casualties. After two days they had only managed to travel a distance of fifteen miles. When they arrived at the bridge at Parit Sulong they found that it was in the hands of the Japanese who were in well-fortified defensive positions and ably assisted by a machine gun section. Despite Anderson's attempts to dislodge the Japanese from the bridge, he was unsuccessful. By the evening of 21 January, Anderson's column had suffered even more casualties, to such an extent that he sent forward two ambulances full of some his wounded men under a flag of truce, requesting that they be allowed to pass through the Japanese lines to the safety of Allied positions closer to the causeway. Much to Anderson's surprise, not only did the Japanese refuse his request but they demanded that Anderson's men surrender and, by way of a carrot, offered to care for the wounded if the rest of his men surrendered. Anderson refused. Possibly incensed by this, the Japanese refused to allow the ambulances with the wounded on them to be returned back to Anderson's position, going as far as threatening to shoot the wounded should attempts be made to remove them from the bridge. However, two of Anderson's wounded men managed to retrieve the two ambulances and remove them from harm's way.

Anderson's men received some help the following morning in the shape of the Royal Air Force who bombed the Japanese-held end of the bridge, but to no avail. The Japanese were still there holding their position and preventing Anderson and his men making good their escape. Later that morning Anderson gave the order for all of his remaining able-bodied men to make good their escape through the jungle the best way they could, and make their way to the safety of the British lines at Yong Peng. This also meant having to leave behind some 150 wounded men who simply could not be moved unaided and certainly not with any kind of speed.

Anderson reasonably assumed that the Japanese would care for his wounded men – how wrong he would turn out to be. According to Colin Smith's 2006 book, *Singapore Burning*, an estimated 145 of them were murdered by the Japanese, with only a handful managing to escape. There were reports of them being bayonetted, machine gunned, set on fire, and many of the Indian prisoners being beheaded.

Lieutenant Ben Hackney and Private Reginald Wharton were the only white Caucasian men to survive the massacre and both subsequently gave evidence at the war crimes trials that were held in Singapore.

The Japanese soldiers who were responsible for the massacre at Parit Sulong, were from the Imperial Guards Division of the Japanese Imperial Army; their commanding officer was General Takuma Nishimura. When General Percival surrendered to General Tomoyuki Yamashita on 15 February 1942, Nishimura was placed in control of the eastern half of Singapore during which time what became known as the Sook Ching massacre took place, when Japanese secret police murdered thousands of Chinese males. After the war, Nishimura was tried and found guilty by a British military tribunal in Singapore, but only in relation to the Sook Ching massacre and not the Parit Sulong massacre.

# CHAPTER FIVE

# BATTLE OF SINGAPORE

The Battle of Singapore took place between 8 and 15 February 1942 and resulted in a Japanese victory when the British and Commonwealth forces, who were defending the island, surrendered. By the time the battle was over, an estimated 80,000 Allied soldiers walked off into captivity as prisoners of the Japanese. For many this was the beginning of the end, as they did not survive the harsh conditions and the sometimes brutal and sadistic treatment meted out to them by their Japanese captors.

The fall of Singapore went down as the biggest disaster in British military history; never before had so many British-led troops surrendered. Added to the 50,000 British and Commonwealth troops who had been previously captured by the Japanese in nearby Malaya, the British Prime Minister at the time, Winston Churchill, was not a happy man.

Why did Japan invade Singapore? The answer, although not a complex one, is reasonably lengthy. Throughout most of the 1930s Japan had been fighting in numerous different conflicts. On 19 September 1931 they invaded Manchuria immediately after the staged Mukden Incident. They stayed there as an army of occupation until their surrender at the end of the Second World War.

What was known as the Second Sino-Japanese war, which in essence was fought between the Republic of China and the Japanese Empire, began on 7 July 1937 and didn't officially end until Japan finally surrendered on 15 August 1945.

Because of her continued fighting with China, certain Allied nations such as the United States, the Soviet Union and Great Britain, all of whom supported China in her struggles, placed trade embargoes on Japan in an effort to get her to cease hostilities, but to no avail. Japan had decided upon a course of action that she hoped would ultimately bring her victory in South East Asia and the Pacific.

Although matters had been simmering in the region for some time, they literally exploded in a global sense on 7 December 1941 when the Imperial Japanese Navy attacked the United States Pacific Fleet at its home base at Pearl Harbor in Hawaii. Although the attack was a resounding Japanese victory, it was ultimately a decision which four years later would lead to their total and absolute downfall and defeat.

The Japanese attack at Pearl Harbor caught the Americans by surprise. By the end of the onslaught, eight of their battleships were badly damaged or sunk, and eleven other ships were also damaged. On top of this, 188 of their aircraft were destroyed and a further 159 damaged. Their total casualties were 2,403 sailors who were killed and another 1,178 who were wounded.

The very next day Japan carried out simultaneous attacks on Malaya, Hong Kong, the Philippines and Thailand, all countries which had close links with Britain, especially when it came to trade and raw materials.

# CHAPTER SIX

# LIEUTENANT ADNAN BIN SAIDI

Adnan bin Saidi is regarded as a true hero by both Malaysians and Singaporeans alike.

Adnan was born in Sungai Ramal, a small village in the State of Selangor, which is situated on the west coast of what in 1942 was Malaya. Like Adnan, two of his brothers, Ahmad and Amarullah, also served in the military during the Second World War. Amarullah fortunately survived, and as recently as October 2014 was living in Kajang, which is close to the village of Sungai Ramal.

Ahmad, who was an Ordinary Seaman (SE/X658) in the Malayan Navy, was recorded as missing presumed killed in action when the ship he was on, HMS *Pelandok*, was attacked on 9 December 1941 while it was on its way to Australia. It was part of the Malayan Naval Volunteer Reserve.

Adnan was a married man. His wife, Sophia Pakir, was an intelligent woman, a teacher by profession, who taught Islamic religious education. Adnan and Sophia had three children, two sons, who still live in Malaysia, and a daughter, who died very soon after she was born. Sophia passed away in 1949.

Adnan was a career soldier, having joined the Royal Malay Regiment at its inception on 1 March 1933. One thousand applicants applied to join the newly formed regiment, but so high was the standard required that only twenty-five were accepted for what was at the time still only an experimental unit. By 1 January 1935 the experiment to see how Malaya's young men would deal with the trials and tribulations of military discipline was over. There were now 150 young men who 'had what it took' to become soldiers.

Originally the Malay Regiment only had the one battalion, but their numbers were growing all the time, and by 1 January 1938 they had increased in size to nearly 800 officers and men. They were an extremely professional body of men, especially for such a young regiment. They had a machine gun platoon, a Bren gun carrier platoon, and two rifle companies, as well as having been trained in the use of mortars and anti-tank weapons.

With unrest increasing in the area, the regiment had the raising of a second battalion approved by the Governor of the Strait Settlements in March 1941. It would be the first of the Regiment's battalions to have the opportunity to show what they were capable of, when 'A' Company engaged the Japanese after they had made an amphibious landing at Kampung Salak. Though they fought bravely they were forced to retreat due to overwhelming enemy numbers.

On 13 February 1942 at about 1400 hours, the 18th Division of the Imperial Japanese Army attacked Allied defensive positions which consisted of soldiers from 'B' Company, 1st Battalion, Malaya Regiment, who had been strategically positioned along the Pasir Panjang Ridge, at what is today known as Kent Ridge Park. The Japanese infantry had the added advantage of having the support of both artillery and tanks. The Japanese were unstoppable as well as brutal in their application of modern warfare.

Despite 'B' Company's heroic efforts to thwart the advancing Japanese, they did not prevail. When their ammunition ran out, rather than give in they resorted to hand-to-hand fighting with fixed bayonets rather than capitulate and surrender. They were surrounded by the Japanese; if they were going to die, it was going to be honourable death. They were proudly led by Captain Yazid Ahmad, who was subsequently killed during the fighting. Most of the men of his company were either killed outright, some were captured and taken prisoner of war, while a few of them managed to make good their escape.

The following morning at about 0830 hours, the determined and battle-hardened Japanese attacked again, this time with all their might, including the added support of both artillery and mortar fire. So sustained was their attack that the Malayan defenders had to fall back and take up a new defensive position at a location known as Bukit Chandu.

The Malay soldiers were heroically led in their final stand against the Japanese at Opium Hill by Second Lieutenant Adnan bin Saidi of 7 Platoon, 'C' Company, the 1st Battalion, Malay Regiment. To a man they put up an extremely brave fight against a fearsome enemy. Eventually they ran out of ammunition but rather than take the easier option and surrender, they chose to engage in hand-to-hand combat with their attackers.

Adnan bin Saidi, although badly wounded, was one of only a handful of Allied soldiers who were still alive at the end of the fighting.

He was taken prisoner by the Japanese, but rather than treat him with honour and respect for the brave manner in which he had personally fought and led his men, they reportedly tied him to a tree and bayoneted him to death.

The significance and importance of Bukit Chandu, for both sides, was that behind it was the Alexandra area of the city which was now open and undefended to the advancing Japanese. It contained the British Army's main ammunition and supply depots on the island as well as being the location of Alexandra Military Hospital.

In just two days of heavy fighting, between 12 and 14 February 1942, the Malay Regiment lost a total of 159 officers and men killed, and many more who were wounded or captured in their efforts to valiantly defend Singapore, in spite of the fact that Percival subsequently surrendered the island so readily the very next day.

The body of Adnan bin Saidi was never recovered by the Allies, with some reports claiming it had been burnt by the Japanese. His name is commemorated on the Singapore Memorial which stands in the grounds of the Kranji War Cemetery, which is situated on the north side of the island overlooking the Straits of Johore, the waters which separate Singapore and Malaysia.

In total the memorial contains the names of 24,000 Commonwealth servicemen who died either during the Malaya campaign and the defence of Singapore, or after these events due to their wounds, disease, or illness. It was unveiled by the then Governor of Singapore, Sir Robert Black, on 2 March 1957.

# CHAPTER SEVEN

# ALEXANDRA MILITARY HOSPITAL MASSACRE

One of the outcomes of any war is that people die, both military personnel as well as civilians, and this includes individuals who should never have been killed. But during the Second World War the Japanese carried out so many abhorrent atrocities, they took levels of wanton brutality and lack of humanity to entirely different levels.

Nowhere was this highlighted so vividly than when they murdered fifty unarmed and defenceless soldiers and hospital staff at Alexandra Hospital, and then returned the following morning and murdered another 150. The sick were lying unarmed and defenceless in their beds, still having their wounds treated.

Alexandra Hospital was originally called the British Military Hospital, first opening for business in 1938, and served as the main medical facility for British forces throughout the Far East. It remained in this capacity until 1971, when it was handed over to the Singaporean Government for civil use.

On the afternoon of 14 February 1942, with Britain close to surrendering to the quickly advancing Japanese forces, Japanese soldiers under the overall command of General Tomoyuki Yamashita arrived at Alexandra Hospital. The horrors which were about to unfold could never have been thought possible. From time immemorial a hospital, no matter where its location on the battlefield, has been seen as a kind of sanctuary where wounded and sick men from either side could expect to receive kindness, compassion and the same level of medical care no matter which side they were on. That's obviously not quite how the Japanese saw it.

Part of the Wikipedia page that covers the Battle of Singapore includes an entry concerning the Alexandra Hospital massacre. In it is the following sentence:

*A British Lieutenant, acting as an envoy with a white flag, approached the Japanese forces but was killed with a bayonet.*

Records show that there were in fact fourteen lieutenants serving in the British Army who were killed in Singapore on 14 February 1942, two of whom were members of the 32nd Company, Royal Army Medical Corps. They were Lieutenant Geoffrey G. Rogers and Lieutenant William Frederick Jayne Weston, both of whom were killed at the Alexandra Military hospital.

William, or Billy as he was known to his family, had only become a lieutenant in the Royal Army Medical Corps the previous year. As Japanese soldiers approached the rear of the hospital, Lieutenant Weston, clearly holding a white flag of truce, walked towards them, but before he could say anything, a Japanese soldier ran him through with a bayonet. As he lay dying on the ground the Japanese soldiers simply stepped over him and quickly made their way into the hospital.

On entering, the Japanese soldiers set about indiscriminately killing doctors, nurses and patients alike, basically anybody they came across, showing none of them any mercy.

At least one soldier, Corporal (3384885) Gerald Holden, from the 2nd Battalion, the Loyal Regiment (North Lancashire), who was undergoing surgery at the time of the attack, was killed while lying on the operating table. In his anaesthetised state, it is doubtful that he would have felt any pain as the Japanese bayonet, which ended his life, entered his already limp and lifeless body. He is buried at the Kranji War Cemetery along with 4,460 Commonwealth servicemen from the Second World War, 850 of whom still remain unidentified.

Before ceasing their crazed onslaught, the Japanese soldiers rounded up an estimated 200 members of staff, tied them up, and left them overnight in some of the hospital's outbuildings. The following morning the Japanese soldiers returned to their tired, hungry and terrified captives and proceeded to shoot and bayonet them. It is estimated that some 200 male staff and patients died as a result of this action.

While this horror was going on, Japanese shells started to rain down on the hospital causing a sufficient distraction to allow a handful of prisoners to escape unnoticed. Four who are known to have survived were George Britton of the East Surrey Regiment, Private Haines of the Wiltshire Regiment, and Hugo Hughes and George Wort, both from the Royal Malay Regiment.

The big question which is always asked in relation to the Alexandra Hospital massacre is, why did it take place? Many theories have been put forward, the most widely accepted suggesting that Japanese soldiers were responding to being shot at by retreating Indian troops who had been firing at them from or near the hospital. Personally I don't see how that version has much strength as an argument, as it surely must have been blatantly and immediately obvious to them that those they were killing in the hospital were not Indian soldiers.

In my opinion the most likely explanation is that they simply wanted revenge for their friends and comrades who they had lost in fierce and bloody fighting on their way through both Malaya and Singapore.

At the subsequent war crimes trials which began in Singapore on 21 January 1946, nobody was ever brought to justice for carrying out the atrocities which had taken place at Alexandra Hospital. Nobody disputes that it actually took place, but with a lack of witnesses who were able to identify those responsible, sadly there was little else that could be done.

Lieutenant General Tomoyuki Yamashita, who was in command of the Imperial Japanese 25th Army on Singapore up until 17 July 1942, was tried for war crimes, found guilty and hung on 23 February 1946 at Los Banos prison camp, south of Manila, after having been found guilty by an American military tribunal which had lasted from 29 October to 7 December 1945. He was found guilty in relation to atrocities in both the Philippines and Singapore. These included the Sook Ching and Alexandra Hospital massacres, even though he wasn't present at either and no documents ever came to light connecting him to either event. The main accusation was that he had failed in his duty to control the troops under his command by preventing them from carrying out the massacres.

It has to be remembered that war crimes trials were a relatively new phenomenon. They and the terms and conditions which went with them had not been used for some twenty-five years. There was the added crossover of military law against civil law and which held precedence. The case against Yamashita caused a certain amount of controversy; it certainly set a precedent in relation to the responsibility that went with being in command, and not surprisingly, in the circumstances, became known as the Yamashita standard.

The legitimacy of the trial was questioned by some, based on various procedural matters, the allowance by the court of hearsay evidence as well as other evidence which suggested that in relation to the Philippines Yamashita did not have ultimate command responsibility over all military units. Even two American Supreme Court judges stated that the trial was a miscarriage of justice, a denial of basic human rights, and no more than an exercise in vengeance by the Americans.

So as to be fair and unbiased on this matter, it is only right and proper to point out that in relation to the Alexandra Hospital massacre, Yamashita had the officer in charge of the troops who carried out the attack, along with those soldiers who engaged in looting while in the hospital, executed. He also personally apologized to the surviving patients.

# CHAPTER EIGHT

# THE BATTLE BOX

In some respects, the 'Battle Box' is a slightly unusual name for what was in fact a large communications and command bunker. It was built underneath Fort Canning in Singapore between 1936 and 1938 for all British military operations in the Far East, and to conduct strategic planning in the event of war. It is situated in a hilly location at a central point of the island. After Singapore became a crown colony in 1867 a fort was built, Fort Canning, but by the turn of the century the structure had become surplus to requirements as other defences, which had been built elsewhere around the island, reduced its level of importance and necessity.

It has to be said that it is an extremely impressive structure, but for anybody who has actually been inside its innermost sanctums, they will know that it can leave you with mixed feelings. For the claustrophobic, I would respectfully suggest it would not be something you would put at the top of a bucket list of must-do things before you die.

Once you step inside those impressive steel front doors, there is a small flight of five steps. Once up these, the terrain flattens out for about ten yards, and then your world suddenly changes as you start your descent into the heart of the bunker. The first thing you notice is the disappearance of the gentle breeze that was apparent when you first stepped inside. You are suddenly hit by the heat and the humidity of the place – it almost takes your breath away.

Once you get down to the lowest level the humidity really starts to make an impact. The perspiration is by now dripping off you as if you have just stepped out of a shower.

The main walkway is about six feet wide with rooms off both sides. The walls which separate the rooms from the corridor are three feet thick. Walking from one end to the other it almost feels like a prison.

The more people present in the Battle Box, the more humid would the atmosphere have become. Humidity is a part of everyday life in Singapore, no matter what time of the day or night it is, or whatever time of the year. It is not a country of seasons with winter, spring, autumn and summer; it has a rainy season and a time when it isn't the rainy season. Being incarcerated in a concrete bunker thirty feet underground must have been like sitting in a sauna while sun bathing on a hot summer's afternoon.

The longer you stay in the Battle Box the worse it becomes. It gets harder and harder to breath and the perspiration stings your eyes as it drips down from your forehead – and this is just on a normal day as a visitor, some sixty years after the war ended. Add to this already energy-sapping atmosphere, the elements of fear, trepidation and apprehension, the constant threat of Japanese artillery shells and their aircraft bombing the bunker at will, and it must have been an extremely uncomfortable experience for the British officers and men who were enclosed within it.

The 'air conditioning' system, or what passed for it, was primitive to say the least, certainly when compared with today's standards. What the bunker actually had was a recycling air supply system. It became so stifling and overbearing at times that the men who were working there regularly had to go up to the surface to get some much-needed fresh air and to be sick. Just being in that environment was difficult enough, but these men also had to be able to think, concentrate, and remain calm whilst making extremely important decisions.

Officers were trying to keep an up-to-date picture of what was actually going on in Singapore. They needed to know exactly where the Japanese forces were at any given time, so that they could try to counter them as expediently as possible. One of the problems for the British was the unprecedented speed with which the Japanese managed to move their forces forward; it was akin to a 'Blitzkrieg'. Add an element of indecision, possibly disbelief and maybe a bit of arrogance on the part of the British, and it made for a difficult time.

The decision to surrender to the invading Japanese forces was taken at a meeting which commenced at 0900 hours on 15 February 1942. Lieutenant Colonel Percival, General Officer Commanding, Malaya, had called the meeting of his senior officers to consider their options. The feedback wasn't good. The talk was of retreating Allied soldiers who were being constantly forced back by an ever-advancing and determined enemy.

By 0930 hours the decision to surrender to the Japanese had been made. Later that day they left the Battle Box for the last time and made their way to the Ford Factory at Bukit Timah to meet with the Japanese. They took with them a white flag of surrender and a Union Jack.

Soon after the surrender officially came in to place, the Japanese took over the Battle Box and it then became the headquarters of Major General Kawamura, and his staff.

# CHAPTER NINE

# BRITISH SURRENDER AT SINGAPORE

The four-man British delegation that made their way slowly yet purposefully to the Ford building for the formal surrender meeting consisted of Captain Cyril Hew Dalrymple Wild, a Japanese-speaking staff officer who carried the white flag on the day; next to him was Brigadier T.K. Newbigging, the Chief Administrative Officer, Malaya Command, who carried the Union Jack flag; Brigadier K.S. Torrance, General Staff Malaya Command; and Lieutenant General Arthur Percival. They were joined on their way to the surrender ceremony by Lieutenant Colonel Ichiji Sugita of the Japanese Imperial Army who was the official Japanese interpreter at the surrender ceremony.

When the Japanese had declared war on Great Britain in December 1941, General Archibald Wavell was made Commander in Chief of the American-British-Dutch-Australian Command (ABDACOM). With the Japanese already having entered the island of Singapore, the following cable was sent to Wavell on 10 February 1942 from Winston Churchill, with whom he didn't have a particularly good relationship, letting him know in clear and unequivocal terms what he expected of the troops and officers under his command:

*I think you ought to realise the way we view the situation in Singapore. It was reported to cabinet by the Chief of the Imperial General Staff that Percival has over 100,000 men, of whom 33,000 are British and 17,000 Australian.*

*It is doubtful that the Japanese have as many in the whole Malay Peninsula. In these circumstances the defenders must outnumber the Japanese forces who have crossed the Straits, and in a well contested battle they should destroy them. There must at this stage be no thought of saving the troops or sparing the population. The battle must be fought to the bitter end at all costs. The 18th Division has a chance to make its name in history. Commanders and senior officers should die with their troops. The honour of the British Empire and of the British Army is at stake. I rely on you to show no mercy to weakness in any form. With the Russians fighting as they are and the Americans so stubborn at Luzon, the whole reputation of our country and our race is involved.*

*It is expected that every unit will be brought in to close contact with the enemy … and fight it out.*

This was the same message that Wavell then passed on to Percival before he left for Java on the evening of 10 February 1942, so that everybody was absolutely clear what was expected of them. So quick was the Japanese advance that the likelihood of having to fight to the very end was becoming greater and greater.

Despite Churchill's instruction, the situation on Singapore Island was becoming almost untenable. All remaining Air Force personnel were ordered to the Dutch East Indies where it was believed they would be of better use. All Allied airfields throughout Singapore had either been captured or were so badly damaged from the almost incessant Japanese air raids that it was no longer possible to get any British aircraft into the air.

There was a large British military petrol depot near to the village of Bukit Timah and, rather than let it fall in to the hands of the advancing Japanese, Percival ordered that it should be set on fire, as the very idea of it falling into the hands of the Japanese wasn't one that he seriously wished to contemplate.

The defence of Singapore quickly became a fast-moving and fluid situation which was rapidly changing for the worse. Plan 'A' would quite often become outdated before it could even be implemented, adding to the trauma for Percival, with Churchill's words of 'fight on to the very end' constantly ringing in his ears like a bad case of tinnitus.

Percival showed his human side even in the midst of a desperate battle to save the island. He was genuinely concerned for the wellbeing of the female nursing staff, having heard what had happened when the Japanese had overrun Hong Kong and savagely raped nurses there. He did not want the same fate to befall the nurses of Singapore should they fall in to the hands of the Japanese, so he ordered they were all to be evacuated. The Japanese air force did all they could to stop anybody escaping from Singapore and did not differentiate between naval and civilian shipping. Any vessel seen leaving the island's docks was deemed to be fair game and was attacked accordingly.

Percival seemed to be constantly having to juggle his responsibilities. One minute he was considering his military options and what units he could put where to deal with the latest Japanese attack, and the next minute he was having to concern himself with the food situation both for his men and the population at large. If it wasn't food, it was water. If it wasn't water it was ammunition. If it wasn't ammunition it was whether or not to burn the island's currency reserves, when he should pour away all of the island's alcohol, and whether or not he should blow up Singapore's radio broadcasting station to make sure it didn't fall in to enemy hands.

As the Japanese had fought their way down the Malaya Peninsula, so a wave of refugees had moved before them and had ended up inside the perimeter of the city of Singapore. This had increased the population dramatically which in turn had put more strain on the food and water that was available.

The constant Japanese air raids and artillery bombardments that were aimed at the city around the clock were having a massive effect on the civilian population, which in turn had put a massive strain on the island's hospitals. It was estimated that the civilian death rate had reached 2,000 each day, with similar numbers being wounded by collapsing buildings or fires.

The last thing Percival needed was for the thirteenth of February 1942 to be a Friday, but it was. That evening it had been decided that the remaining fifty or so ships and boats in Singapore Harbour would be used to get as many people out of Singapore as was possible, with particular priority being given to the last of the nurses.

By 13 February it was fair to say that the situation on Singapore had become dire for Percival and his men as the Japanese came nearer and nearer to victory. As Percival now saw it, he was left with two options: launch an immediate counter-attack, or surrender. After a meeting with his commanders it became clear from what he was hearing that the able-bodied troops which he had left under his command were close to physical and mental exhaustion, greatly reducing any realistic opportunity to undertake a decisive counter-attack. His only other sensible alternative therefore was to surrender.

Immediately after the meeting with his commanders he sent a cable to General Wavell requesting that he be given discretionary powers should he feel the need to surrender to avoid an orgy of violence and torture being committed against his troops, as had occurred after other Japanese victories in the region.

Wavell's reply would not have been the one he was hoping for:

> *You must continue to inflict maximum damage on the enemy for as long as possible by house to house fighting if necessary. Your*

*action in tying down the enemy and inflicting casualties may have vital influence in other theatres. Fully appreciate your situation but continued action essential.*

On the morning of Sunday, 15 February 1942, Percival held another meeting with his military commanders, the Inspector General of Police, representatives from Civil Defence, as well as the Water Engineers, so as to gain an overview of the current position. His mind was made up as to what he had to do, maybe helped to some degree by another cable which he received from General Wavell, which although encouraging him to keep on fighting, also gave him the discretion to capitulate when he was satisfied that it was not possible to continue the defence of the city any longer.

Whether either Wavell or Percival knew how many Japanese they were up against at the time is not recorded, but the chances are that they wouldn't have known until much later. If they had have known for certain the numbers they were up against, how might that have changed the outcome at Singapore and the war in the Pacific as a whole?

# CHAPTER TEN

# BANGKA ISLAND MASSACRE

This chapter is about the brutal and horrific murder of twenty-one Australian nurses at Radji Beach, Bangka Island, on the morning of 16 February 1942, the day after the surrender of Singapore by the British.

In the aftermath of the surrender of Singapore, hundreds of frightened evacuees were making their way to the docks area of the city to try to find a place on a ship so that they could escape from Singapore before the Japanese took over from the British, leaving everybody who remained behind with an uncertain future.

Amongst the large throng of people who were trying to make good their escape were sixty-five nurses who were members of the Australian Army Nursing Service from the 2nd/13th Australian General Hospital which had been situated on the island. The group's two senior matrons were Olive Paschke and Irene Drummond. The ship on which they had managed to get spaces was the coastal freighter the *Vyner Brooke*, one of nearly fifty ships that managed to sail in the days before Singapore fell. The ship, which was captained by Richard Borton, set sail without too much fuss and excitement, but unfortunately it wasn't to remain that way for long. The *Vyner Brooke* had only made it as far as the waters off Banka Island near Sumatra and Borneo when she was attacked by Japanese bomber aircraft, even though she was obviously not a naval type vessel.

The small, defenceless ship, with nowhere to hide and in open waters, was struck by the falling bombs. Besides the nurses and other able-bodied personnel, also on board were numerous wounded Allied servicemen. The *Vyner Brook* sank within a half hour of being hit. Two nurses were killed as a direct result of the ship being bombed and another forty-one drowned when the ship went down. Twenty-two of the Australian nurses survived by finding their way to the island of Bangka after drifting at sea, some of them for days. Those who made it to the ship's lifeboats were continuously strafed by Japanese aircraft. Initially it was not appreciated by the survivors that the island was already occupied by the Japanese, but when it was, one of the survivors, an officer from the crew of the *Vyner Brooke*, walked into Muntok, one of the towns on the island, with a group of women and children and in effect surrendered them to the authorities.

The nurses had stayed on the beach to tend the wounded who had managed to survive the sinking. Later the same morning, the ship's officer returned to the beach with a Japanese Army officer and about twenty of his men. All of the wounded who were able to walk were shepherded around a nearby headland. Once out of sight, the nurses heard shots ring out. The Japanese soldiers then returned to the beach and sat down in front of them, fresh blood clearly visible on their bayonets.

Next, the nurses were ordered into the sea by the Japanese officer, Captain Orita Masaru, who ordered his men to shoot them. They died in a hail of bullets from a machine gun that had been set up on the beach. The remaining wounded soldiers who had not been able to walk were then bayoneted to death on the stretchers upon which they lay, defenceless.

The gruesome events of that morning only became known because one of the nurses, although badly wounded, managed to survive. She was Nurse Vivian Bullwinkel who, covered in blood from her own wounds, feigned death and remained up to her waist in the sea until the Japanese soldiers had left. The bullet that hit her went through her hip. Fortunately, like Nurse Bullwinkel, many of Captain Masaru's troops could not swim, so they did not venture into the surf to check that everybody was in fact dead.

Later that day her limp and bloodied body was washed up on the beach. Once she had worked out where she was, she discovered a wounded British soldier, Private Patrick Kingsley, who somehow, like her, had survived the massacre. She would later describe what happened:

> They started firing up and down the line with a machine gun. They just swept up and down the line and the girls fell one after the other. I was to the end of the line and a bullet got me in the left loin and went straight through and came out towards the front. The force of it knocked me over into the water and there I lay. I did not lose consciousness, the waves brought me back on to the edge of the water. I lay there 10 minutes and everything seemed quiet. I sat up and

*looked around and there was no sign of anybody. Then I got up and went up in the jungle and lay down and either slept or was unconscious for a couple of days.*

She and Kingsley managed to stay at large for twelve days, she tending to his wounds and doing her best to keep him alive. Before long they both realized that if they wanted to stay alive, they had to give themselves up to the Japanese and hope for the best. Despite their trepidation, they handed themselves in, saying that they been shipwrecked. Thankfully their story was believed. They were placed in separate camps; but unfortunately Private Kingsley died of his wounds a few days later.

She made no mention of the earlier incident on the beach, and fortunately nobody recognized her as having being there. Much to her surprise, she discovered twenty-four other Australian nurses (or perhaps it was twenty-two – the numbers are uncertain) who had been on the *Vyner Brooke* when she was sunk and who had been washed up on another part of the island, already in the camp.

She spent the next three years in the camp, and proved strong enough to survive the starvation and disease that sadly killed many of her friends and colleagues in captivity. Out of the original sixty-five nurses who had left aboard the *Vyner Brooke* from Singapore, only twenty-four of them eventually managed to complete the journey, which took them nearly four years.

After the war, Vivian Bullwinkel was able to bring to light the truth about the murders of her twenty-one fellow Australian nurses on Radji Beach on that horrible day in February 1942.

The memories of that day must have been extremely painful for her, standing in the surf of the waves up to her waist, having already heard some of her fellow survivors being shot and killed, to then be stood in a line with a group of friends, knowing that each of them would soon be dead. The word brave doesn't properly describe Vivian Bullwinkel.

In 1993, along with friends and colleagues, she returned to the very same beach on Bangka Island, where she had been shot all those years ago for the unveiling of a memorial to the nurses who were murdered and to those who died. She died on 3 July 2000, aged 84.

Twenty-one Australian nurses, whose job it was to tend the sick and wounded in the hope that their efforts would help to save lives, were murdered in cold blood by Japanese soldiers on that fateful day in February 1942, and it is only right and proper that their names are therefore remembered. Their names are:

Matron Irene M. Drummond

| | |
|---|---|
| Sister A.M. Beard | Sister B.L. Keats |
| Sister A.J. Bridge | Sister J. Kerr |
| Sister F.R. Casson | Sister M.E. McGlade |
| Sister F.R. Cuthbertson | Sister K.M. Neuss |
| Sister F.L. Balfour-Ogilvy | Sister D.G.H. Elmes |
| Sister I.F. Fairweather | Sister F.A. Salmon |
| Sister P.E. Farmener | Sister E.S.J. Stewart |
| Sister C.I. Halligan | Sister M.M.A. Tait |
| Sister N. Harris | Sister H. Wilmott |
| Sister M.I. Hodgson | Sister H.J. Wright |

Their names are commemorated on a plaque on the Remembrance Wall near to the Cenotaph in Paterson Street, Launceston, Tasmania. The plaque was unveiled in 1964 by Colonel John Edis, Indian Medical Service (retired), who was the Director General of Health Services in Tasmania.

# CHAPTER ELEVEN

# THE SOOK CHING MASSACRE

The Chinese words 'Sook Ching' translated into English is, 'a purge through cleansing,' and that's exactly what it was. For the Japanese the operation was known as Kakyou Shukusei.

There is no dispute that the massacre took place, but both Japan and Singapore significantly disagree as to the numbers of those who were killed.

It occurred over a two-week period between 18 February and 4 March 1942, and was overseen by the feared Japanese secret police, the Kempeitai.

Its background lies in the history of the two nations and the conflict which had beset them for many years. The Japanese and the Chinese had been involved in the First Sino-Japanese War from 1 August 1894 to 17 April 1895. This had been fought between the Qing Dynasty which controlled China and a Japan that was led by Emperor Meiji, and was mainly over control of neighbouring Korea. In the end Japan won the day, with China eventually having to sue for peace.

The Second Sino-Japanese War, which began in 1937, didn't officially end until Japan's final capitulation in September 1945, so when they arrived in Singapore on 15 February 1942 they knew that the Chinese population of the island were loyal to either Great Britain or to China, and as such were a potential threat to them. Some of the wealthier Chinese had organised fund-raising events, and the monies raised were then sent to China to help finance the National Revolutionary Army.

Japan would have known that she faced opposition from within certain elements of the island's civilian population long before her troops had arrived in Singapore.

When exactly is not clear, but this wasn't just a sudden or random last-minute idea; it had been thought through, and was, I would suggest, planned well in advance of the Japanese arriving in Singapore. Their leaders had drawn up a list of individuals who they classed as being 'undesirables', which included the following:

- Activists in the China Relief Fund
- Wealthy Chinese who had made donations to that fund

- Supporters of Tan Kah Lee, leader of the Nanyang National Salvation Movement
- Those perceived to be communists
- Those born in China and who came to Malaya after the start of the Second Sino-Japanese War
- Tattooed men, which at the time suggested membership of a Chinese Triad
- All Civil Servants
- Those who joined the Singapore Overseas Chinese Anti-Japanese Volunteer Army
- Anybody who had a firearm

It was one thing to have a list of those who were classed as being undesirables, but locating all of these individuals was going to take a lot of time, work and effort. To achieve their goal they set up 'screening centres' all over the island where Chinese males aged between 18 and 50 had to come forward and register. Those who were believed to have anti-Japanese tendencies were arrested, taken away to different locations around the island, and murdered.

The following passage is taken from an article from the National Heritage board of Singapore:

> *The inspection methods were indiscriminate and non-standardised. Sometimes, hooded informants identified suspected anti-Japanese Chinese; other times Japanese officers singled out 'suspicious' characters at their whim and fancy. Those who survived the inspection walked with 'examined' stamped on their faces, arms or clothing; some were issued a certificate. The unfortunate ones were taken to remote places like Changi and Punggol and unceremoniously killed in batches.*

In total there are eleven killing sites that are known of, where these executions took place.

The first of these locations was at **Changi Beach**, with the killings taking place on 20 February 1942, just five days after Singapore had been surrendered to the Japanese. A total of sixty-six Chinese males from the Bukit Timah/Stevens Road locality were lined up and shot dead by the Kempeitai.

**Hougang** reportedly saw six lorry-loads of people murdered. The exact number of those on the lorries is not known, but an estimate of each lorry having twenty-five people on board gives a figure of at least one hundred and fifty.

The **Punggol Beach** massacre took place on 28 February 1942 and saw between 300 and 400 Chinese males from the Upper Serangoon Road shot by units of the Kempeitai.

The **Changi Road** massacre took place in a nearby plantation area. A later search of the area found the remains of 250 victims.

The **Katong** massacre site covered an area big enough to cater for twenty trenches. It is not known how long or deep they were, so trying to guess at the numbers of victims who were buried in them is difficult.

The **Amber Road** massacre or, to be more precise, the beach opposite number 27 Amber Road, saw two lorry loads of Chinese males murdered at that location.

**Tanah Merah Beach/Tanah Merah Besar Beach saw** 242 Chinese males from the Jalan Besar area murdered there. The location of the massacre later became part of the Changi airport runway.

The **Sime Road** massacre saw an unspecified number of victims found in numerous sites close to that area.

The **Katong, East Coast Road** massacre saw a staggering 732 Chinese males from Telok Kurau School murdered at this location.

The **Siglap** area massacre saw an unspecified number of victims murdered at that location.

The **Blakang Mati Beach** massacre didn't actually take place at that location; it happened somewhere out at sea and the bodies then washed up on the beach at Sentosa. British prisoners of war were given the unenviable task of burying some 300 bullet-ridden corpses that were washed up at Sentosa.

The Japanese Government later admitted to having murdered some 5,000 Chinese males, while the Singaporean Chinese community claim there were anywhere between 50,000 and 100,000 young men who were systematically murdered as part of the Sook Ching massacre.

Looking at the known massacre sites in more detail we know that six of the locations saw 1,990 murdered. Two of the locations involved a total of eight 'lorry loads' with a conservative guess that each lorry contained 25 people, which provides for another 200 people. One of the massacre sites had twenty trenches dug and filled with murdered Chinese males. If 50 victims were buried in each trench that would mean another 1,000 dead. The numbers murdered at the remaining two massacre sites are not certain.

From the identified massacre sites it can be established that a minimum of 3,190 victims were murdered.

In January 1947 the war crimes trials began in Singapore, but only seven Japanese officers were put on trial for the Sook Ching massacres. They were Lieutenant General Takuma Nishimura, Lieutenant General Saburo Kawamura, who was in charge of Japan's Singapore garrison, Masayuki Oishi, who was the Lieutenant Colonel in charge of the Kempeitai in Singapore, Yoshitaka Yokata, Major Jyo Tomotatsu, Major Satoru Onishi and Captain Haruji Hisamatsu.

The main issue for the prosecutors was the lack of a paper trail of evidence against any named individuals. Not one document was found that was signed by any of the accused connected to the Sook Ching massacre, which made it extremely difficult to prosecute all of those who were in the dock.

Two of the accused who were found guilty, Oishi and Kawamura, were handed the death penalty and were hanged on 26 June 1947, the remainder received life sentences. The main part of each man's defence was that they were 'just following orders'. How a soldier of any rank can be lawfully ordered to murder an innocent civilian or an unarmed prisoner of war by a senior officer is one thing, but for them to then be able to use the defence that they were 'just following orders' surely does not seem credible?

After Nishimura had served only four years in Changi prison he was sent back to Tokyo to finish off the remainder of his sentence. He was sentenced to life imprisonment but was released from prison in Singapore after having served only four years, and sent back to Tokyo to serve the remainder. On his way back to Japan, the ship he was on docked at Hong Kong. While there, it was boarded by Australian Military Police who proceeded to forcibly remove Nishimura from the vessel. He was then placed before an Australian Military Court on Manus Island in Papua New Guinea to face charges in relation to the Parit Sulong massacre. He was found guilty for ordering the shooting of wounded Australian soldiers, and the subsequent desecration of their bodies at Parit Sulong. He was also found responsible for the deaths of 110 Australians and 35 Indian prisoners after the Battle of Bakri. He was sentenced to death by hanging; the execution was carried out on 11 June 1951.

It later transpired that the Australian Army prosecutor in the case, Captain James Godwin, had been mistreated by the Japanese while being held as a prisoner of war in Sumatra. At Nishimura's trial, Lieutenant Fujita Seizaburo claimed that it was he who had ordered the Parit Sulong massacre, but he was neither arrested nor charged in relation to the incident.

Sosaku Suzuki died before he could be charged with war crimes. He was promoted to the rank of lieutenant general in March 1941 and in November 1941 he was reassigned to the Japanese 25th Army under General Tomoyuki Yamashita and was in Singapore certainly up to the early part of February 1942. By October 1944 he was the commander of the Japanese 35th Army and charged with defending the southern part of the Philippines against the Americans. He was killed on 19 April 1945 when a boat he was trying to escape on was attacked by American aircraft. How much involvement he had in the Sook Ching massacre is unclear.

Colonel Masanobu Tsuji was surprisingly never tried for any war crimes and died of natural causes in Laos in 1968 aged 68. His main role during the Second World War was as a tactician in the Imperial Japanese Army. He was largely responsible for coming up with the operational plans for the successful invasion of Malaya. It later came to light that he was either involved in or contributed to the murders carried out during the Sook Ching massacre, as well as the infamous Bataan Death March which began on 9 April 1942 on which many Filipino and American prisoners of war died or were murdered on a forced sixty-mile march. When Japan surrendered, fearing he would be arrested for war crimes, Tsuji went in to hiding in Thailand and China, only returning to Japan in May 1948 when he finally felt it was safe to do so. He then wrote a best-selling book about his years of hiding in Thailand.

Otani Keijiro was a lieutenant colonel in the Kempeitai during the occupation of Singapore. He confirmed the wartime atrocities that had been carried out on the island by Japanese forces during the Second World War and condemned his countrymen for their actions. As he was in charge of the Jalan Besar screening centre at the time, it would be almost inconceivable that he did not know what the men under his control and command were doing which, if he did, would make him just as culpable as them for their actions.

# CHAPTER TWELVE

# SINGAPORE IN THE EYES OF THE PRESS 1942–45

A great deal of history going back many years has been recorded in both national and local newspapers, but then sadly forgotten about. Fortunately, a great many of these newspapers have been digitised in recent times and made available for future generations to peruse at their leisure.

The *Dundee Evening Telegraph* of Friday, 6 February 1942, just nine days before the surrender of Singapore by the British Army to the Japanese, printed the following article in its newspaper:

### Singapore, 'As strongly defended as Britain.'

*The Singapore Free Press quotes a senior British officer as saying, 'Yard for yard, I think Singapore Island is every bit as defended as Britain.'*

One can only assume that the unnamed officer was either attempting to keep morale as high as possible amongst the local population because he knew of the islands impending fate, or he genuinely didn't have any understanding of the predicament he was soon to find himself in.

The following detailed report on the rapidly deteriorating situation in Singapore appeared in the *Evening News* on Thursday, 12 February 1942:

### Japanese tanks pressing on Singapore line.
### Enemy claims unconfirmed
### Surrender call rejected

*Japanese forces on Singapore island are using light and medium tanks in considerable numbers in an effort to break British resistance on a line running roughly from north to south through a point about five miles from the centre of the city.*

*Latest information reaching London gives this as the position which has been stabilised at 4.30 GMT yesterday, which is about midnight in Singapore, and although other news from reliable sources is scarce, there is no apparent justification for wild axis claims that the Japanese are fighting in Singapore.*

It was extremely difficult for the British authorities to confirm initial reports of Japanese advances in Singapore as they were relying greatly on press releases, not all of which were unbiased, or were connected in some way to either official Japanese or German news agencies. The situation was made even more confusing by the statement made by Lieutenant General Sturdee, the Australian Chief of Staff, when he informed the Army Minister, Mr F.M. Forde.

*There were such strong forces and ample supplies in Singapore that the Japanese claims to have captured the city were incredible.*

*The forces there would put up as good a resistance as General MacArthur is doing in the Philippines.*

It would appear that the press reports were a lot more accurate than anything senior British or Commonwealth officers were saying about the situation, as the reality was that by 12 February 1942 Japanese forces had already reached the south-west area of the town and were making their way into the city centre, and that although British resistance was still very strong, it was eventually overcome in the face of Japanese aggression.

The main thing that took most observers totally by surprise was the speed with which Japanese forces progressed down the Malaya peninsular to their eventual victory in Singapore. The situation was undoubtedly made even worse by an apparent misjudgement on the part of the British high command as to just how efficient an enemy they were up against.

The *Derby Daily Telegraph* for Thursday, 12 February 1942, carried the following report:

### Singapore Battle nears heart of the City: Thunderous duel of big guns.

*The battle lines of Singapore moved steadily towards the heart of the city today after a night of heavy artillery fire on both sides. Shells exploded continuously in the northern part of the island. Bitter counter attacks by British infantry, supported by a powerful artillery barrage, last night drove back the enemy at several points north of Singapore.*

On the same day the following report appeared in the *Daily Express*:

### Singapore: The Last Stand
### Percival ignores Jap note by air:
### 'Lay down your arms'
### Fierce Street Battles

*British troops are this morning fighting to the end in the shelled and bombed suburbs of Singapore City against tank and Tommy gun infantry onslaughts. Another Japanese note calling on General Percival to surrender has been ignored.*

*News of the British defiance was given in a Singapore communique which reached London late last night, breaking an official silence of 36 hours.*

*It admitted that the Japanese were driving fiercely on the city, their tanks being supported by bombers and fighters.*

*The surrender demand was made at 7.30 in the morning. According to a Tokyo communique, the Japanese, at 8 o'clock, entered the city 'after breaking desperate resistance.'*

*It added the claim that 'remnants of the British troops are now being mopped up.'*

*Japan's capital immediately began to celebrate the fall of the city. But later Tokyo radio spoke of fierce hand to hand fighting in the streets.*

*The spokesman said that the battle was 'not yet over,' adding that it was anticipated that the main clashes between the Japanese and British Empire troops would take place 'in the southern part of the island.'*

### Sea of Flames

*The Singapore communique said: 'The enemy drive from the west has been directed on Singapore City, and has been pressed with vigour during the night. In addition there has been some infiltration today.*

*The enemy advance has been assisted by tanks and considerable bomber and fighter support, and our troops covering the west sector have been forced further back.*

*At 7.30 this morning a Japanese note was dropped by air addressed to the High Command asking for the unconditional surrender of our entire forces. No reply has been made to this note.*

*In the western and north-western sector, bitter fighting continues. In the east of the island enemy activity has been slight.*

*Tokyo indicated that the Singapore City battle is going on in a sea of flames. The railway station, Keppel Harbour, and several districts in the western part were reported to be ablaze.*

It was interesting to note that two British national daily newspapers were reporting the same fighting, but in a totally different way, to such a degree that it almost did not appear to be the same incident that was being reported on.

On 16 February 1942, the day after Singapore had fallen to the Japanese with the surrender of the island by British and Commonwealth forces, the following article appeared in the *Hartlepool Mail*:

### Singapore

*The fall of Singapore opens up grave possibilities like the breach in a mighty dam. It makes easier the Japanese possession of all the Far Eastern islands. It brings the threat to Australia closer than ever. Thus, also, it opens the way to Japanese invasion of the Indian and South Pacific oceans, and materially aids the Japanese attempt to deny us our communications in those waters. Negatively, it adds months if not years to the war by compelling us, in the absence of the Singapore base, ultimately to creep forward by slow process and over a long period from island to island which Japan rushed in a few weeks.*

*The alternative to this is retaking Singapore by land. But Mr Churchill has frankly declared that the situation has resulted in great part from a disbelief that Japan would be so mad as to go to war with the English speaking nations. This disbelief of course has affected our preparations in Burma and the alliance with China is new. In these circumstances land operations must be in the farther, rather than in the immediate, future. Japan, also in possession of Malaya and Singapore, will be ready for land attacks as we were not. So in any case, as we have indicated, the Pacific war must be more prolonged than if Singapore were still ours.*

*In this interval we must be prepared to experience many more bad moments such as that which is now ours. We, our Australian and New Zealand kin, our Indian associates and our Dutch allies have to recognize this. But there is one fact to hold on to grimly through all the trials yet to come. It is that it is only a matter of time before Japan goes down; the time required to gather our united strength and deploy it and use it.*

*The political implications attending Singapore and other recent events we leave to the House of Commons. Obviously the efficient conduct of the war is gravely challenged. It is for the House to hear Mr Churchill, as the public heard him last night, and then to express its views and will on behalf of the country. We may then have a new start with a reorganisation of the directive machinery which will have*

*happier results than shown in Crete, Libya, and Malaya; more appro-
priate to the joint might of four of the greatest countries in the world.*

With both Malaya and Singapore having already fallen to the
fast-moving Japanese Army, there were real concerns that Australia
and New Zealand would soon suffer the same fate. There was the
added belief that, although the Allies would eventually retake the
island state of Singapore, this wasn't something that was going to happen any time soon.

On Monday, 16 February 1942, the following article appeared in
most of the daily newspapers throughout Britain:

### Singapore Surrenders
### Documents signed in Ford works
### Cease Fire sounded in Malaya

*British forces on the beleaguered island of Singapore surrendered to
the Japs yesterday at 7pm Singapore time. A party of four British
officers headed by Major Wilde, a member of the British Army Staff,
approached Japanese Army headquarters bearing the white flag of
truce at 2.30pm, and notified the Japanese authorities of the readi-
ness of the British forces to surrender.*

*The British and Japanese commanders-in-chief, Lieut.-Gen.
Percival and Lieut.-Gen. Yamashita, met in the Ford Motor plant
at the foot of Bukit Timah hill and signed the surrender documents.*

The battle for Singapore had taken the Japanese less than a week
to win. The first sight of Japanese forces on the island had been on
Sunday, 8 February, when their troops landed on the north-west of the
island across a ten-mile stretch. The British were taken by surprise as if
it was an attack they had never expected to come from where it did. It
had always been believed that any attack by the Japanese would come
from the sea and not the land.

Somewhat bizarrely, one of the terms of the surrender was that
1,000 armed British soldiers would remain in Singapore City to maintain order until Japanese soldiers arrived to complete the occupation.

The *Daily Telegraph and Morning Post* for Monday, 16 February 1942,
had the fall of Singapore as its lead story:

### Premier announces fall of Singapore.
### Appeal for spirit of 1940.

*The fall of Singapore was announced by Mr Churchill in a broadcast
last night.*

> He described the loss of the great naval base and fortress, which cost £30,000,000 to construct, as a 'heavy and far reaching military defeat.'
>
> Up to a late hour no details of the capitulation were issued in London. A Tokyo communique declared that the Imperial Forces surrendered unconditionally at 7pm Singapore time, 1230pm British standard time.

The *Yorkshire Evening Post* of Saturday, 21 February 1942, had the following article on its front page:

### Jap booty at Singapore

*Japanese headquarters announced that they have taken prisoner 73,000 British soldiers.*

*Booty captured consisted of 300 guns of various kinds, 2,000 machine guns, 50,000 rifles, 200 tanks and other armoured cars, 10,000 cars, 200 motor cycles, a steamer of 10,000 tons and three tankers of 5,000 tons as well as many other smaller ships and enormous quantities of war material and munitions.*

*'Among the British prisoners,' it was added, 'are 8,000 wounded who are at present receiving medical attention. As regards Japanese losses, about 3,000 soldiers were killed or wounded since landing on the island of Singapore.'*

*Berlin Radio, quoting Tokyo reports, today said that in addition to Lieutenant-General Percival, British GOC in Malaya, three other Generals were also prisoners in Singapore.*

The above article was extremely interesting when looking at the official reasons given by the British authorities for the surrender of Singapore. It was said that because of a distinct lack of food, water, petrol and ammunition, senior British officers had no alternative but to surrender to the Japanese, rather than fight to the last man as they had been instructed to do by Prime Minister Winston Churchill.

The British had supplies of oil on the island which they chose to set fire to rather than let fall into the hands of the Japanese. It was slightly confusing that despite confirming that they had taken prisoner 73,000 British soldiers, the Japanese only recovered 50,000 rifles. They also claimed to have recovered enormous quantities of ammunition, despite the British saying that was an item they were close to running out of.

Water and electrical installations were also noted by the Japanese as being in good condition when they took over the island.

Although some ships did manage to leave Singapore with civilian evacuees and RAF personnel right up to the day before the Japanese arrived on the island, there was no British plan or policy in relation to the mass evacuation of her troops, mainly because of Winston Churchill's earlier instruction, coupled with his intention and belief that soldiers on Singapore would fight to the very last.

There was a lot of talk about a Royal Commission enquiry into what had happened at Singapore. Churchill said 'no' at the time as there was neither the time nor the men available, while fighting was still going on in other theatres. Even after the war, successive governments, both Labour and Conservative, did not see fit to hold such an enquiry. Why is not known, but one thing is for certain: if there had been such an enquiry, Churchill's actions and those of his government concerning what they did or didn't do in relation to the Singapore situation would have been in the public domain, warts and all.

Churchill ultimately did not believe that Japan would be as bold as to go to war with either Britain or the United States of America, let alone both of them. That being the case, the question has to be asked: was enough done in the defence of Malaya and Singapore? In the years before the Second World War a lot of work was done on improving the naval facilities on the island in an attempt to make it impregnable, but all of this would appear to have been undermined by a poor defensive strategy, indecisive leadership and an apparent belief that the Far East and Pacific regions had less significance than other theatres of war.

The *Yorkshire Evening Post* of Tuesday, 10 March 1942, had on its back page a small article about one of its own:

### 'Evening Post' man safe

*Mrs K Gillin, of 20 Buckingham Road, Doncaster, wife of Leading Aircraftsman Joseph Gillin has received a cable from her husband who is safe in India.*

*A few weeks ago Mrs Gillin received news that he had arrived in Java from Singapore, where he had been for some months. Leading Aircraftsman Gillin was on the editorial staff of the Evening Post in Leeds until he joined up.*

The *Yorkshire Evening Post* of Friday, 17 July 1942, included the remarkable story of a soldier's escape from Singapore after the surrender of the island, in a stolen Sampan:

### Tin hat exchange for fruit
### How Goole soldier escaped from Singapore

*A thrilling account of how he escaped from Singapore after the surrender by sailing for seven days in a sampan with two companions who knew nothing of navigation, is given by Bombardier Derek Buttle (22), in a letter to his parents, Lieutenant-Commander D H Buttle RNVR, and Mrs Buttle, Airmyn Avenue, Goole.*

*He writes that after the cease fire he saw a chance of escape by making for Sumatra in a small boat. He tried to 'sign on' a crew, but none of his friends would risk it. However, he found an officer and another soldier who were prepared to try it.*

*They started up an abandoned ambulance and tore through the town, 'a ruin of debris, shell holes, burnt out cars and tangled tramlines.' The Japs spotted them and opened fire with mortars, but they got through to the waterfront. There they helped themselves to a Sampan.*

### Three days without food

*Their troubles soon began. They could not make headway against a strong tide and fell asleep exhausted, only to find when they woke up that they were six miles out, for the tide had turned. With a small sail made from flour sacks, and a compass found among the wreckage of a ship, they set course, sailing by night as Jap planes swept the skies by day.*

*On a small island they traded their tin hats to a native for tinned fruit, biscuits and coconuts, their first meal for three days.*

### Lucky mistake

*Morro Island was their next call and they were helped by a Chinese dentist, himself evacuated from Singapore. He gave them some Chinese clothes and they had good reason to be thankful for them as they were mistaken for fishermen by a Japanese patrol boat.*

*After seven days they reached Dutch territory, and were later taken to India by a British warship.*

*Bombardier Buttle adds that he is still a little bewildered, and wonders why he was so favoured by good fortune.*

The *Yorkshire Evening Post* from Wednesday, 1 July 1942, included an article on page six which seemed to be extremely harsh to say the least. It was about disgruntled wives of serving soldiers:

### Will this happen?

*Mr R R Stokes (Labour Ipswich) is to ask the Secretary of State for War, 'whether he is aware that wives of men of the 4th Suffolk Regiment, captured at Singapore, have been notified that their allowances will be reduced as from August 2, 1942, unless further news is received of the men in the meantime, and whether this is the policy which he intends to pursue with all the dependants of captured or missing persons.*

It would appear that this couldn't have been a very widespread policy as captured soldiers were still paid their wages for the time they spent in captivity, although they would have had to have waited until they were returned to British control before being able to collect their backdated pay. With this in mind it would appear inconceivable that wives' allowances would be reduced while their husbands were being held in captivity.

The *Yorkshire Evening Post* for Friday, 4 December 1942, covered a story about Allied leaders who were being held captive by the Japanese:

### Allied leaders in Jap hands
### Messages broadcast from Tokyo

*Messages from Lieutenant-Colonel Percival, Commander-in-Chief of the British Forces in Malaya, and Sir Shenton Thomas, Governor of Singapore, now interned by the Japanese, were broadcast by Tokyo radio.*

*They were among a number collected by a Japanese correspondent visiting the camp.*

*General Percival's message, addressed to Mrs Percival at Heath Gate, Hertford Heath, Hertfordshire, read:*

*I despatched a long letter three weeks ago. I have not heard from you for a year. Try to cable via the Red Cross, Geneva. I was moved north in August and am now accommodated in wooden buildings in a good climate. The minimum winter temperature is 50 degrees. I have as recreation reading, gardening and cards.*

*I have sufficient warm clothing. If you are sending a parcel include socks, scarf, thick shirt, condensed foodstuffs, books and cards.*

*I am spending little money here, so draw freely on my account.*

*Best love to …*
*Father, Margery, James, yourself and others.*

Sir Shenton Thomas's message was to his daughter, Mrs Ernest Lotinga, at Woodlands Cottage, Englemere, Ascot, Berkshire. He said:

> *I have been transferred to a prisoner of war camp in a cool healthy climate. I am quite well. I sent you a postcard in the middle of June and a letter in the middle of October. I want news of you.*
>
> *Ask Cator, of Malaya House, to consult the Red Cross and the British Broadcasting Corporation about the best way of cabling to me, and also to Mother if she is not yet with you.*
>
> *Fondest love to all. Always thinking of you. Don't worry. Have a happy Christmas. Inform family and Colonial Office, Daddy and Grandfather.*

Mail, or rather the lack of it, appeared to be a common theme for both men. Not to have heard from a loved one for so long, especially in those somewhat unique circumstances, must have been difficult for even those blessed with an inbuilt mental strength. Alone with their own thoughts, thousands of miles from home in a prisoner of war camp, not knowing if or when they would return home, must have been a continual discomfort.

The *Yorkshire Evening Post* of Wednesday, 29 December 1942, included the following story about a one-legged pilot from Singapore:

### One legged RAF Pilot

> *Flight Lieutenant T R Byrne, AFC, of Amersham Bucks, who lost a leg in the Far East fighting, is flying again in defence of England.*
>
> *Born and educated in Singapore, as well as being educated in England, he helped defend Singapore against the Japanese. He has just joined an active spitfire wing stationed in the south after taking a refresher training course. His leg was amputated early last year after his aircraft had been bombed by Japanese at Sumatra.*
>
> *Byrne who is 23, has flown more than 1,300 hours since he joined the RAF in 1938. Leaving Singapore 11 days before its fall, he went to Sumatra and flew Hudsons on coast patrol duties.*
>
> *Flight Lieutenant Byrne is now with the wing which scored the highest number of enemy aircraft destroyed in the whole of Fighter Command during September.*

The *Yorkshire Evening Post* Tuesday, 14 December 1943, contained an article from a Captain Gammans, who one assumes was retired as he was also the Conservative Member of Parliament for Hornsey, North London. He was talking about a letter he had received from an unnamed friend of his who at the time was in Chungking in Southwest China, who had managed to escape from Singapore:

**A Japanese massacre**

*When the Japanese entered Singapore, the first day they killed 5,000 of our people. On the second day they divided Singapore into several sectors, and got all our people into the streets for checking.*

*They were left in the open three days and three nights without food and shelter.*

*Five men were chosen by the Japanese to scrutinise the people, to find out whether they were anti-Japanese. They sat with their faces covered at a table, and by simply nodding their heads sent people to their fate.*

*Then over 50,000 young men and women were taken to an unknown destination. Not a single one has come back.*

The article didn't clarify if the man who had sent the letter had actually witnessed what he had written about, or whether it was what he had been told by others who had. The killings he was referring to were undoubtedly the Sook Ching massacre. One assumes that title had not yet been attributed to the killings in December 1943.

The *Yorkshire Post and Leeds Intelligencer* dated Wednesday, 20 June 1945, reported on the belief that Japanese forces might be about to abandon Singapore as the outcome of the war was looking more and more likely to be a defeat for Japan:

**Japanese might abandon Singapore**
**Heavy traffic up the Malay Peninsula**
**Tokyo Invasion Warning**
**Battle for Okinawa nearly over**

*The possibility that the Japanese may withdraw from the Singapore area to avoid being cut off there is suggested by reports of unusually heavy railway traffic north along the Malay Peninsula towards Bangkok, capital of Siam.*

*[That the] Japanese fear an early Allied invasion of the homeland was emphasised last night when a Tokyo broadcast to the nation forecast that Japan would be invaded within the next few months.*

*Allied reports indicate that the battle for Okinawa, the island which may be the springboard for invasion, has virtually reached its end. Japanese troops are fleeing towards the cliffs on the last corner of the island they hold.*

*The blockade of Japan is tightening rapidly. A Tokyo broadcast admitted last night that Allied submarines had penetrated into the Sea of Japan in minelaying operations, and were working in conjunction with minelaying Super Fortresses.*

The *Lancashire Evening Post* of Saturday, 11 August 1945, carried the sad story on its front page of a soldier who had died in November 1942 and the man's parents had only just been informed by the War Office of their son's death.

### Died in Jap camp

*News has been received through the War Office that Gunner V Bellis, eldest son of Mr and Mrs I T Bellis, Promenade, Southport, died in a Japanese prisoner of war camp in November 1942, from dysentery and malaria. He joined the Royal Artillery at the outbreak of the war, and after being captured at Singapore, the only news received from him was a postcard stating that he was a prisoner.*

The *Hull Daily Mail* of Thursday, 16 August 1945, carried a report on its front cover concerning the Japanese surrender, after Emperor Hirohito had ordered his armed forces to lay down their arms and cease hostilities immediately as of 1.30 am British Standard Time:

### Surrender ceremony in Singapore

*Arrangements are being made to accept the local surrenders of Japanese commanders at Rangoon and Singapore.*

*It is understood that one of the conditions which will have the strictest enforcement, calls on the Japanese to hand over installations intact. Area commanders who do not comply will be shot.*

*The surrender ceremony in Singapore will be no harsher on the Japanese than that imposed on the British when the enemy humiliated the losers in February 1942, in a patient effort to degrade the white man in the eyes of the Malayans. In fact the Japanese protocol is expected to be carried out in reverse.*

*The most immediate problem is the handling of the estimated 75,000 Allied prisoners in Singapore. All prisoners of war will be taken to their home countries as soon as they can be moved.*

*It is estimated the surrendered Japanese in south-east Asia and the Indies total 800,000 to 900,000 men. There is no intention of moving SEAC headquarters soon to Singapore but a small forward headquarters will be established there immediately.*

The *Hartlepool Mail* of Friday, 31 August 1945, included a report about the preparation for the re-occupation of Singapore:

### Singapore
### Preparing for the re-occupation

*A Reuter report from Fleet HQ says that a mine-sweeper force of the British East Indies Fleet was getting ready at the northern end of the Malacca Strait to begin the work of clearing a passage through the minefields to Singapore. The minesweepers will be prepared for any hostile action.*

*A Japanese News Agency dispatch from Singapore said that the Japanese inhabitants there are busily devoting themselves to various tasks in their pre-arranged place of concentration at Julong, about 12 miles west of Singapore.*

*The dispatch added, 'It is undeniable that the pro Japanese atmosphere has vanished from the city, though so far no act of violence or sabotage by the natives has been reported.'*

*A radio message from SEAC HQ to the Japanese commander at Singapore said, 'You will arrange immediately reception for the dropping of POW and internee parcels on airfields in Sumatra from Monday.'*

*Plans for the surrender of 38,000 Japanese troops, scattered over 100 islands of the Truk group in the South Pacific were made today on board an American warship. It was agreed that the final papers shall be signed on Sunday, reports Reuters from Guam.*

*Heading a five man Japanese delegation, was Rear-Admiral Michio Sum Kawa, Chief of Staff of the Japanese Fourth Fleet. Marine Brigadier Leo D Hermle, deputy commander of Guam, led the American group.*

The *Lancashire Evening Post* of Saturday, 1 September 1945, reported the release of a large number of Allied prisoners of war in Singapore:

### Over 20,000 captives freed at Singapore
### They include 6,500 British servicemen

*More than 20,000 Allied prisoners of war and civilian internees have been released from five camps in Singapore by a relief party dropped from the air, New Delhi radio said today.*

*They included some 6,500 British soldiers, marines and airmen, and more than 5,000 men of the Australian Army.*

*Previous reports from the relief team had stated 1,808 officers and 14,477 other ranks of all the Services and the Allied merchant marine, 399 civilians were contained in four of the 23 camps on the island.*

*The Japanese estimate that there are all together 30,500 prisoners on the island. Allied forces will begin landing in the Singapore area after the signing of overall surrender terms in Tokyo, a Japanese News Agency report said today.*

*The Singapore Public Services Association has issued instructions that Japanese residents are to complete their evacuation of five areas by this evening, according to the Japanese News Agency today.*

*At least 23,000 out of 30,000 American troops in the Far East at the outbreak of the war died, most of them in Jap prison camps, from brutality, neglect and sadistic medical experiments, said a US Doctor, Mack Gottleib, on board the US hospital ship, Benevolence, today.*

*Dr Gottleib, who was captured at Guam, spent the entire war in Japanese prisoner of war camps. He said he was unable to estimate the additional thousands of Navy, Marines and Air Force men who died.*

### Prisoners Tortured

*The Japanese prisoner of war authorities inflicted both mental and physical torture on the Allied prisoners of war and stole Red Cross parcels, he added.*

*American airmen got 'special treatment' from civilians who often beat and tortured them, and then from officials who tortured them for information.*

The *Gloucester Citizen* newspaper dated Thursday, 6 September 1945, reported the following:

*The famous Fifth Division has taken over Singapore from the Japanese. Indifferent to Japanese Military Policemen still directing traffic, the local population is thronging the streets, expressing its jubilation.*

*The life of the city was normal until three days ago, when business houses closed, but they will soon be open again. There had been no organised looting or rioting after the Japanese had evacuated into the suburbs.*

*Alan Humphreys, Reuters special correspondent in Singapore, cabled today: 'Singapore was like a ghost city when I landed with the first party ashore.*

*'The streets were deserted and all shops and buildings closed and shuttered with an occasional Japanese sentry standing with a fixed bayonet.*

*'Outside the Raffles Hotel, I met the first two of many British strollers. They were Mr A Breade, whose wife is in India, and Mr F V Lucock, whose wife is in Australia. Both had been civilian internees since the capitulation.'*

*Former employees of the British Government were reporting for duty in Singapore today and the occupation was progressing a good deal faster than had been expected, said Singapore radio.*

*The British military authorities have already taken a number of measures to restore efficient administration in the city. The Japanese still at large have been ordered to gather in the football ground.*

*All persons have been asked to retain their Japanese identity and ration cards as well as other registration documents. There is a fair amount of British currency in circulation, and the unofficial exchange rate is 40 Jap dollars to £1.*

After three years of what history tells us was a sometimes brutal Japanese occupation, life in Singapore quickly began to revert back to some kind of normality, with Englishmen strolling at their leisure around the streets, taking in the warmth of the afternoon sun, while armed Japanese soldiers were still openly in their midst. A surreal situation for all concerned, but a reminder of just how quickly fortunes could change.

The *Lancashire Evening News* for Monday, 10 September 1946, carried the following story:

### Singapore Ceremony

*General Itagaki, Japanese Commander at Singapore, is to take the place of Field Marshal Terauchi in Singapore surrender. Admiral Mountbatten has made it quite clear that Terauchi cannot escape the humility of personal surrender and must present himself at Singapore later.*

Winston Churchill addressed the Houses of Parliament on the still somewhat tender issue of the fall of Singapore. The contents of his speech appeared in the *Yorkshire Post* and the *Leeds Intelligencer* on

Monday, 28 January 1946, under the heading of 'Tragedy of Singapore'.
Here is some of what he said:

> *The tragedy and disaster of Singapore happened against a back-*
> *ground of more than one third of our battle-ships and battle-cruisers*
> *out of action, our forces fully extended to meet the new enemy, Japan,*
> *and America temporarily entirely crippled at sea.*
>
> *After a long rear guard action down the Malaya Peninsula, there*
> *were, according to the War Office figures, about 100,000 men gath-*
> *ered in the island of Singapore by the morning of February 3. On*
> *the night of February 8 about 5,000 Japanese made a lodgement on*
> *the north-west corner of the island, and were gradually reinforced*
> *by landings from other points until perhaps 30,000 men had been*
> *landed.*
>
> *After five or six days of confused but not very severe fighting, the*
> *Army and the fortress surrendered. This episode and all that led up*
> *to it seems to be out of harmony with anything that we have experi-*
> *enced in the present war.*
>
> *I do not wonder that requests should be made for an enquiry by a*
> *Royal Commission, not only in to what took place upon the spot in*
> *the agony of Singapore, but into all the arrangements which had been*
> *made beforehand. I am convinced, however, that this would not be*
> *good for our country and it would hamper the prosecution of the war.*
>
> *Australian accounts reflect upon the Indian troops. Other credible*
> *witnesses disparage the Australians. The lack of any effective count-*
> *er-attack by the 18th Division, which arrived in such high spirits and*
> *good order, and never seem to have had their chance, is criticised. The*
> *generalship is criticised. There is an endless field for recrimination.*

Churchill's reluctance for an enquiry to be conducted by a Royal
Commission into the surprising capitulation and surrender of
Singapore by senior British officers, raises a massive question mark as
to why. Did he and his government have something to hide?

His explanation for not supporting a Royal Commission was weak
at best. The war was over by the time that he made his comments;
the Allies were the victors, so surely the timing was right to explore
all avenues into what went wrong at Singapore in minute detail. An
enquiry isn't necessarily about recriminations, it has more to do with
learning from mistakes and what went wrong at all levels, to ensure
that the same mistakes were not made again. This makes Churchill's
decision not to go ahead with an enquiry difficult to understand.

After the war's end there were still plenty of British servicemen stationed in Singapore. As can be seen by the following article in the *Bath Chronicle and Weekly Gazette* dated Saturday, 31 August 1946, not everything was as harmonious as might have been expected between British military personnel and the local populace. Sapper G.F. Goater, serving with the South East Asia Command in Singapore, and who was waiting to return to England in preparation for his demobilisation, wrote to his father back home in Bath:

> As each ship brings back civilians to Singapore, more and more sarcastic letters appear in the local press, resenting the fact that the Servicemen are remaining here, as if we desired to do so!
>
> There have been letters about service motor transport wasting petrol and also causing accidents, one even went as far as to say that Servicemen are slightly better than the Japs.
>
> We think this is an insult, after so many lives were lost, and so much misery was endured by prisoners of war and after the fighting forces went through hell to regain Singapore, these impertinent scribblers have the effrontery to write such insults.

How horrible it must have been for young British and Commonwealth soldiers to read such comments after everything that they had gone through and the efforts they had made. Maybe those writing the letters were doing so out of bitter memories of the Japanese occupation and a feeling of being let down by their British masters.

CHAPTER THIRTEEN

# RAFFLES HOTEL

It is hard to write a story, any story, about Singapore and not include a piece in it about the world famous Raffles hotel. It was originally owned by the Sarkies brothers, first opening for business in 1887, and is named after the founder of Singapore, Sir Stamford Raffles.

It was built where it was because at the time the sea was literally just across the road from the hotel, so as people alighted from the ships after a long and tiring sea journey, possibly as long as three months if they had sailed from England, they only had to make their way across the road to the sumptuous and palatial surroundings of the waiting Raffles hotel, which was the epitome of British colonialism.

Sometimes at high tide the sea would calmly and slowly make its way uninvited across Beach Road and into the hotel's foyer. The entrance area at the front of the hotel was subsequently raised slightly to prevent this from happening.

During the Japanese occupation of the Island, which began on 15 February 1942, the hotel was used as the headquarters for the Transport and Supplies Section of the Japanese Imperial Army while high-ranking officers lived in the hotel's relaxing rooms, ate in its restaurants and drank at its bars, enjoying all that the hotel had to offer as much as they possibly could. To give it a more homely feeling they even renamed it 'Syonan Ryokan,' which literarily translates as 'Light of the South Hotel'.

After the Japanese had surrendered to the Allies in August 1945, their accommodation became somewhat less salubrious. The officers who had enjoyed the hotel's splendour, some for over three years, were moved out of the Raffles hotel and into prisons which were dotted all around the island, most of which were tented affairs.

The following article appeared in the *Picture Post*, dated 14 February 1942, the day before the surrender of Singapore to the Japanese:

> *Places of entertainment are certainly conspicuous in Singapore town. The Cathay Cinema is one of the biggest blocks on the land-scape, and the Victoria Theatre towers over the new Government offices. At night time China Town comes to life, and then you can go to Chinese cabarets, Chinese cinemas, or Chinese restaurants. If you*

*want to dance, you hire a partner, or 'Taxi Girl,' at four dances a dollar. At Peng Hock and Shaw's New World Cabaret you buy your four tickets in a little book and everyone is inscribed, 'Good for One Dance Only.' NB, Coupons not bearing the Chop of the Managing Director, Mr Ong Peng Hock, are not valid.*

*Of the hotels, the Adelphi, Sea View, and Raffles are the places to go to when you are on leave. Sea View is actually five miles from the town, in a coconut plantation on the sea front, and its swimming pool is protected from sharks by reinforced concrete. At the Raffles they still talk of Charlie Chaplin and Paulette Goddard calling, on their honeymoon, and of Noel Coward's conversation at cocktail time, but most of all about a legendary character called Two-Gun Cohen, who was employed as a bodyguard to a Chinese General and was always ready to bet he could shoot a hole in a penny thrown up to the ceiling.*

*In Singapore town you see plenty of imitations of the European style, and the law courts, for instance, are almost a replica of the Old Bailey*

Over the years, certain stories have been promulgated about the Raffles Hotel during the Second World War and the island's occupation by the Japanese. One of these was that when Japanese soldiers arrived at the hotel in February 1942, they found a group of European guests dancing one final waltz before being taken in to captivity and an uncertain future. Myth or fact? More likely to be a combination of the two, as the hotel was certainly a central meeting place for ex-pats from both Britain and Europe. When news about the possibility of Japanese soldiers making their way in to the city broke, ex-pats congregated in the hotel. Some in disbelief at what they hoped would never happen, some for re-assurance and some simply for a drink with their friends.

Supposedly, expensive items of silverware were buried in the hotel's gardens to save them falling in to the hands of the Japanese.

Another story goes that some 300 Japanese officers killed themselves at the hotel after the surrender to the Allies, by blowing themselves up with grenades. It is well documented that Japanese officers and soldiers would commit suicide over a matter of honour, but the preferred means for doing this was by the act of Hara Kiri, where they would disembowel themselves with a razor-sharp knife called a *tanto*. Yes, it is quite feasible that a few Japanese officers did commit suicide in the Raffles Hotel at the end of the war, but I would suggest that it is extremely doubtful that there were 300 of them who used grenades to do it.

At the end of the war and with Japanese officers no longer occupying the hotel, it was taken over for a period of time by the British military authorities and used as a transit camp for British soldiers who, prior to their release by the Japanese, had been held in captivity as prisoners of war throughout the region and were now in Singapore waiting their turn to be sent back home to Britain. This included those who had been held at Changi and other prisoner-of-war camps across the island. The hotel was finally handed back to its owners after the last of the prisoners of war were finally repatriated in 1947, once again allowing the Raffles Hotel to return to normal and its former glory.

# CHAPTER FOURTEEN

# THE INTERNATIONAL RED CROSS – WARTIME

In August 1948, at the XVllth International Red Cross Conference, held in Stockholm, the International Committee of the Red Cross (ICRC) produced a report covering its activities for the period 1 September 1939 to 30 June 1947. Volume one covered what it called 'General Activities'. The following is taken from that report.

At the outbreak of war between Japan, Great Britain and the United States of America, the ICRC invited the governments of each country to send them all the information they had in relation to captured prisoners of war, so that it could be held at the Central Prisoner of War Agency in Geneva. There was a slight hiccup with this proposal, in so far as Japan had not actually signed or ratified the 1929 Convention in relation to the care of prisoners of war.

It was January 1942 before Japan responded to the ICRC's request, agreeing to inform the Central Prisoner of War Agency in Geneva about all prisoners of war as well as civilian non-combatants they had detained. They also announced the opening of an office in Tokyo of their own Prisoner of War Agency, the *Huryyojohokyoku*.

The ICRC were still keen to illicit from the Japanese exactly how they intended to treat prisoners of war and civilian internees detained by them. Eventually after much pushing by the ICRC, the Japanese Government in Tokyo responded in clear and precise terms.

> *Since the Japanese Government has not ratified the Convention relative to the treatment of prisoners of war, signed at Geneva on July 27 1929, it is therefore not bound by the said convention. Nevertheless, in so far as possible, it intends to apply this convention, mutatis mutandis, to all prisoners of war who may fall into its hands, at the same time taking into consideration the customs of each nation and each race in respect of feeding and clothing of prisoners.*

The phrase *mutatis mutandis* is Latin for, 'the necessary changes having been made'.

Japan also agreed to treat non-combatant civilian internees the same as they would prisoners of war, but their mistrust of all foreigners who were not nationals of a power in allegiance to Japan meant that they were more likely to suspect them of espionage. Even the ICRC's delegation was deemed by both the Japanese civilian and military police to be untrustworthy. They went so far as to regard the delegation as a centre instructed to obtain information for the representatives of the Protecting Power, whose duty was, so the Japanese authorities thought, to establish liaison with Japan's enemy.

The attempts by the ICRC's agents to work with the Japanese Government sometimes placed them in extremely perilous circumstances. An example of this was Dr Matthaeus Vischer, who had been chosen by the Red Cross to carry out their work in Borneo before the island was occupied by the Japanese. When they did in fact invade Borneo in March 1942, the head of the ICRC's delegation in Tokyo was instructed to have Dr Vischer accredited to the authorities and to the Japanese Red Cross. The Ministry of Foreign Affairs in Tokyo, and the Japanese Legation at Berne, were notified of Dr Vischer's presence in Borneo. When renewing its demand that this delegate should be officially recognised by the Ministry of Foreign Affairs, the Committee stated that Dr Vischer's duties in the future would be the same as in the past, namely, 'to care for all the victims of the war in accordance with the tradition of absolute neutrality of the ICRC.'

In spite of frequent applications, the ICRC received no reply from the Japanese until after their final surrender in August 1945. An official of Japan's Ministry of Foreign Affairs verbally expressed, on 18 August 1945, the agreement of the Japanese Government to Dr Vischer's appointment, the timing of which seemed strange and suspicious: a few days previously, the ICRC had been informed by the Swiss legation in Japan that Dr Vischer and his wife had been arrested on 13 May 1943, on a charge of conspiracy against the Japanese Government; they had been tried, found guilty, sentenced to death and executed in December of the same year.

Among the charges brought by the Japanese naval court martial against the Vischers was that of having 'criminally' sought to learn not only the number of prisoners of war and civilian internees in Borneo, but also their names, ages, races, status, conditions of health, and of attempting to send them food which, surprisingly enough, would be exactly what a member of the ICRC would be expected to do in such circumstances. Why Japan's Ministry of Foreign Affairs decided to lie about the Vischers is anybody's guess, especially as the truth of what had happened to them was bound to surface before long anyway.

Unfortunately the ICRC didn't have much in the way of contact with the Japanese Red Cross, who in turn did not have the freedom and autonomy which they had, meaning that there was little if no exchange of information between the two organisations. If the ICRC had been made aware of their plight, this could have proved helpful in relation to the Vischers' situation.

The Japanese Red Cross, which was highly esteemed in Japan, was mainly intended to provide for the upkeep of Red Cross hospitals and the training of nurses. In spite of the best intentions, the 'Foreign Section' of this national society was regarded by the military authorities only as a subordinate department and could not conduct itself in an independent fashion, which meant any communications with them by the ICRC were quite often a fruitless exercise.

Relations with Japan's Prisoner of War Information Bureau didn't fare much better, mainly because they were subordinate to Japan's Ministry of War, which also meant that they could not act independently. During the war, matters became so bad with Japan that the ICRC were requested not to make any personal visits to either agency, but instead to put any questions which they might have in written correspondence.

Late on in the war the ICRC duly sent a note dated 25 April 1945 to the Prisoner of War Information Bureau in Tokyo noting that there was 'a singular lack of information' concerning both prisoners of war and civilian internees who were held in Rabaul, a township in Papua New Guinea. But the directors of the Bureau, who were all retired Army officers and naturally mistrusted all foreigners, took great umbrage at this. Their response was akin to that of a spoilt child throwing a tantrum when it hadn't got its own way. They threatened to stop sending any information concerning the wellbeing or death of prisoners of war to the ICRC in Geneva unless they received an immediate apology.

The ICRC had appointed one of its delegates to Singapore before the Japanese occupation, a Mr Schweizer, by agreement with the island's authorities. A new problem started when the Japanese began their occupation of Singapore, because this meant that the ICRC then had to try to obtain agreement with the Japanese government for official acceptance of the same delegate remaining and working on the island.

Previously the work of the ICRC had been focused on nationals of the Axis powers, but with the outbreak of war in the region, they would now have to turn their attention to prisoners of war and civilian internees from Allied nations.

The problem that the ICRC had in getting Japan to recognise its delegate Mr Schweizer for Singapore was that the Japanese Government had announced that it would agree to the appointment of ICRC delegates in countries it occupied but only if those same countries were no longer regarded as zones of military operations, which at the time Singapore most definitely was. Although the ICRC did not cease in its efforts to have the Japanese Government officially recognise its delegate for the island, they did not succeed. Mr Schweizer was only allowed to carry out his work in an official capacity when Japan surrendered in 1945.

As soon as Japan entered the war, the ICRC wanted to send some of its delegates to the Far East, as the Japanese were coveting their neighbours' lands with alarming speed. Every time the ICRC made an application to the Japanese Government to be able to do this, they were given the stock answer of, 'the time has not yet come to contemplate the carrying out in practice of this scheme.'

The ICRC were hindered by the Japanese authorities at every junction in their efforts to check on the wellbeing of prisoners of war and civilian internees being held in captivity all across the Far East. It was difficult enough for the ICRC to have any of their delegates officially recognised by the Japanese, let alone carry out actual visits to prisoner of war or civilian internment camps.

Even when reports started appearing in British and American newspapers about the 'mistreatment of prisoners of war' or when the words 'massacre' or 'atrocities' were used to describe allegations of wrongdoing by the Japanese, their authorities still wouldn't cooperate with the ICRC.

The Japanese Ministry of Foreign Affairs finally gave its permission for ICRC delegates to visit prisoner of war and internment camps in countries under their control in the autumn of 1943, but for numerous different reasons, relating to travel permits, routes that would have meant travelling through countries at war, availability of transport, and the safety of their delegates, it was June 1944 before an ICRC delegation were able to leave Switzerland to journey to Tokyo, eventually arriving there on 11 August. While the delegation was on route, America had dropped atomic bombs on both Hiroshima and Nagasaki.

Correspondence was another issue, not just because of logistical matters brought about by the size of the theatre of war, but because of mistrust which in turn had led to the Japanese imposing strict censorship on what prisoners of war were allowed to write home to their loved ones. Whether this was to prevent the location of camps being identified or to prevent stories of atrocities becoming widely known is not clear.

The ICRC had conducted negotiations with the Japanese Government over this issue, which led to a 'Declaration of Principle'. Authorities in Tokyo announced that they were 'ready to allow prisoners of war and civil internees to correspond **freely** with their families in foreign countries.' They laid down certain conditions concerning the wording and distribution of messages for the Far East, conditions which the ICRC defined in the following terms in a letter which they sent to the Belgian Red Cross in 1943:

> *The regulations issued by the Japanese authorities limit to 25 words the length of the letters that prisoners of war and civilian internees in the Far East may either receive or send, and require that these letters should either be typed or hand written in capitals. These restrictions are enforced for correspondence addressed to or sent by all prisoners, either in Japan itself, or in Japanese overseas territories, or in territories occupied by Japan. In the case of civilian internees, only letters for those who are in territories occupied by the Japanese forces are subject to these restrictions.*
>
> *For prisoners of war and civilian internees who are presumed to be detained by Japan, but whose names have not yet been communicated, letters may be sent through the ICRC to the Japanese Red Cross. In those cases where the names are known, but the address of their camp is not known, the official information bureau on prisoners of war is responsible for sending such mail through us.*

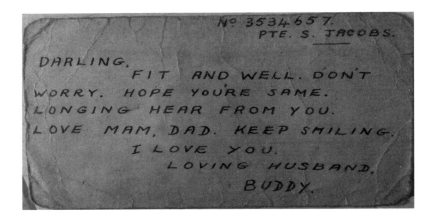

This post card is a good example of the Japanese regulations. Excluding the words which make up the soldier's personal details at the top right of the post card, the message only contains twenty-four words, making sure that other than sending a basic message, there was no allowance for writing anything that could be disparaging about how they were being treated or the state of the camp they were being held in. By ensuring the words were written in capital letters, it ensured that they were clear and precise, and left no room for any ambiguity when being looked at by the Japanese censors.

The card was sent from a prisoner of war camp either in Malaya or Singapore in either 1942 or 1943. Sidney 'Buddy' Jacobs was in the 1st Battalion, Manchester Regiment. Sidney and Bertha had been married in Manchester in 1939, just before the outbreak of the war, but the first of their three children wasn't born until 1947 after Sidney had been released from the captivity of a Japanese prisoner of war camp and repatriated back to England. Sidney's liberation questionnaire shows that he was born on 18 July 1916 and that he joined the Army on 18 April 1940, aged 23, becoming a private. Before the war Sydney's occupation was that of a musician. He became a prisoner of war with the surrender of Singapore on 15 February 1942, at the Changi camp. The British officer in charge of the camp was Colonel E.B. Holmes. He remained at Changi until 30 May 1944 when he was moved to the camp at Kranji where he remained until the end of the war; some 1,000 other men made the same move.

Almost immediately after arriving there nearly all of the men were infested with lice, so every one of them had to have all of their body hair shaved off. The shortage of food was so dire at Kranji that despite having being warned by the Japanese guards not to eat their cats and dogs, on threat of death if they did so and were caught, the pets slowly started to disappear, one by one.

The date of 10 October 1943 was not a good day as far as civilian internees in Singapore were concerned. On 26 September 1943 a group of British and Australian commandos had managed to enter Singapore's main port under the cover of darkness and, with the use of limpet mines, they managed to sink six Japanese ships. It became known as the 'Double Tenth Incident'. On 10/10/1943 the Kempeitai arrested and tortured fifty-seven civilians and civilian internees who were locked up in Changi prison on suspicion that they had somehow been involved in the raid; they hadn't, and nor did they know anything about it. Fifteen of them subsequently died as a result of their torture.

So certain were the Japanese authorities that civilian internees at Changi prison were involved with the harbour raid that they stopped all outside contact with the camp.

In the raid, commandos under the leadership of Lieutenant Colonel Ivan Lyon, part of the 'Z' Special Unit, had sailed from Western Australia in an old Japanese fishing boat named *Krait*. The codename for the Operation was Jaywick. At a predetermined location outside the harbour, the commandos climbed into folding canoes and, as quietly as they could, slowly paddled into the harbour. Once they had set the limpet mines in place, the commandos left as quietly and as unnoticed as they had arrived, rendezvoused with their Japanese fishing boat, and calmly sailed back to whence they had come. The *Krait* has been preserved and is on display at the National Maritime Museum in Darling Harbour, Sydney.

After the war, on 18 March 1946 at Singapore's Supreme Court Building, twenty-one Kempeitai officers and men went on trial, accused of the torture of the fifty-seven internees at Changi prison and the death of fifteen of them.

Lieutenant Colonel Haruzo Sumida was the man in charge of the Kempeitai at the time of the incident, and it was he who was charged by his senior officers with finding out who was responsible for the sinking of the six Japanese ships in Singapore Harbour. Sumida, along with seven of his colleagues, was found guilty, sentenced to death and hung at Changi prison. Three other Kempeitai members were found guilty and sentenced to life imprisonment, another received a sentence of fifteen years, two were found guilty and sentenced to eight-year prison sentences and a further seven were acquitted.

Throughout the war the ICRC representative in Singapore, Mr Schweizer, continued to do his best to assist both civilian internees as well Allied prisoners of war. It was a continuous struggle with the Japanese authorities to allow him to carry on his work.

It is important to remember that in most cases the ICRC only had one representative working in a country, and this was the case in Singapore. Mr Schweizer had to undertake all of the work, whether that was writing letters or reports, visiting locations, attending meetings, making numerous telephone calls or sourcing and purchasing relevant items.

Mr Schweizer had only been appointed on 1 January 1942, but before the British authorities had the opportunity to officially approve the appointment, they had surrendered the island to the Japanese. Because of the suddenness of the change in situation, Mr Schweizer had not been given full instructions from his head office in Geneva as to what it was that they expected of him in his role. He took it upon himself to visit the Town Hall on a daily basis, where the Japanese authorities had put in place a form of civilian government – not one that had any independent powers, of course.

Mr Schweizer was informed by the Japanese that his services as a representative of the ICRC were not required, either for visiting prisoners of war or civilian internees and that under no circumstances would he be allowed to visit any of the camps in which they were being held. Despite this he continued to try to obtain permission to help the civilian internees, but the Japanese authorities refused to change their minds on the matter. He was even forbidden, under threat, from continuing to help in any way, which he had been doing for some weeks by assisting the Australian Red Cross representative. He was not deterred in his efforts to help, managing to purchase some foodstuffs, and was trying his best to retrieve large quantities of medical supplies that had been confiscated by the Japanese, but which in fact belonged to the ICRC. Despite his best attempts his efforts were all to no avail, so he asked that he might be granted a meeting with the Japanese general in charge. He didn't get his requested meeting, instead he got a visit to the local Kempeitai offices, where he was questioned for several hours and accused of spying, more, it would appear, as a scare tactic. He was told in no uncertain terms not to make contact with civilian internees, prisoners of war, or their representatives.

One minute the Japanese appeared to be supportive of what he was doing, or at least didn't stop him from doing it. Then they would change their attitude and would refuse to recognise his status as an ICRC representative but allow him to carry on his work as a private individual, only later to rescind that permission.

Mr Scweizer did his very best to obtain and provide relief supplies for both the civilian internees and the Allied prisoners of war held in Singapore's camps. By the end of the war these supplies had amounted to 2,390,000 Straits Dollars for civilian internees and 117,500 Straits Dollars for prisoners of war, most of which had been provided by the British Government and the British Red Cross. The reason the figure spent on relief supplies for prisoners of war was so much less than that spent on civilian internees is because the ICRC's representative was quite often prevented from providing for them by the Japanese military authorities, camp authorities and the High Military Command, who invariably came up with the same response: 'The prisoners of war are well cared for; they get their pay and consequently need no assistance whatever.' The representative also provided relief for the relatives of the civilian detainees who were resident in Singapore – approximately 5,000 adults and children.

Somewhat ironically, as soon as Japan had capitulated in August 1945, the Japanese Government accorded official recognition to Mr Schweizer in Singapore and he was immediately allowed to carry out visits to both Allied prisoners of war as well as civilian internees, totally unimpeded. Maybe this was with one eye to the future, in the knowledge that their own soldiers were soon to be incarcerated in the same camps and prisons in which they had been the captors.

Once Allied troops had arrived back in Singapore, all Japanese military personnel were interned in camps alongside their senior officers. These camps were immediately visited by Mr Schweizer, who was only too keen to offer his help to the Japanese prisoners of war who were now detained within them without any hindrance or restrictions from the British authorities.

# CHAPTER FIFTEEN

# WAR CABINET REPORT ON THE FALL OF SINGAPORE

As I have already written about earlier in this book, there has never been an official enquiry into what happened at Singapore, either about the weeks and months leading up to the embarrassment of the final surrender in February 1942, or the aftermath of that fateful decision and what happened to scores of Allied prisoners of war and thousands of Chinese civilians who either died of illness, disease or neglect or who were brutalised and murdered by their Japanese captors.

On 25 April 1942 an important meeting took place in London. Those present were members of the War Cabinet of the British Government: the Prime Minister, who would have chaired the meeting, the Air Chief Marshal, the Admiral of the Fleet, the Chief of the Imperial Staff, the Lord Privy Seal, the Chancellor of the Exchequer, as well as secretaries and other personnel.

The meeting was to consider a report on the fall of Singapore. The report was dated 28 February 1942 and was presented by the First Lord of the Admiralty, the Right Honourable Albert Victor Alexander MP, but had originated from the late editor of the *Straits Times* Newspaper in Singapore, Mr George William Seabridge, and had been sent to the Director of British Naval Intelligence, John Henry Godfrey. (As an aside, the fictional figure of 'M' in the James Bond movies was apparently based upon Godfrey by Ian Fleming, who had worked under him in Naval Intelligence).

At the top of the first page of this report was the heading,

<u>**Secret**</u>
<u>**To be kept under lock and key**</u>

It is requested that special care may be taken to ensure the secrecy of this document.

The report was based on notes concerning the Battle of Malaya which originally came from two accredited war correspondents who both worked for the *Straits Times*. What they wrote came from their personal experiences as they made their way back to Singapore from Malaya ahead of the Japanese forces.

It was pointed out that it was not possible at that time to substantiate any of the report's statements, as the editor of the *Straits Times* (Seabridge) had been advised by the British military authorities to leave Singapore at very short notice. He heeded the advice and left Singapore by ship on 11 February 1942 without taking any of the relevant papers or documents with him.

The best I can work out is that he was on board the *Derryman*, a former passenger ship which, when the war broke out, was requisitioned by the Australian Government and became an ammunition ship. Two days into its journey from Singapore to Batavia (now known as Jakarta), and only fifty miles from its destination, it was attacked by the Japanese Kaidal Class Submarine I-55. Although struck by a torpedo it did not sink, but was abandoned. Nine out of the 245 people on board were killed. George Seabridge survived. He returned to Singapore after the war and continued as the editor of the *Straits Times* until 1947, when he retired.

One of those who survived was a wounded Royal Australian Air Force pilot on his way home. His name was John Gorton, and between 10 January 1968 and 10 March 1971 he would be the Australian Prime Minister. Before being rescued by HMAS *Ballarat*, he had spent a day along with other survivors clinging to a life raft in shark infested waters.

The report started by explaining that over the previous few days, two Reuter's articles had appeared in the Colombo (Ceylon) newspapers. One of these messages covered a statement which had been attributed to the General Officer Commanding Malaya, Lieutenant General Arthur Edward Percival. He had allegedly stated that the reason why he felt obliged to surrender Singapore was that he and his men were rapidly running out of food, water, petrol and ammunition. This was not accepted, with the correspondent claiming that there were sufficient food and water supplies on the island to sustain both civilians and military personnel alike for up to six months. In relation to the water supplies he pointed out that there were several reservoirs in Singapore with water reserves that were between eight and twenty feet deep. He also questioned the levels of petrol and oil on the island, pointing to the fact that petrol stocks were so high that Percival had taken the decision to destroy these stocks on or after 12 February 1942.

The report then posed the question that if the statements being attributed to Percival were incorrect, then where did the blame for the capitulation of Singapore actually lie. It went on to suggest that there were four reasons for the collapse and surrender of Singapore. These were:

(1) The almost complete demoralisation of the defending troops.
(2) The striking lack of any offensive spirit.
(3) The widespread acceptance of the view that the Battle for Singapore was a forlorn hope.
(4) In isolated cases, an actual refusal to fight.

The demoralisation came about, the report suggested, because the Japanese Air Force were able to dive-bomb and machine-gun Allied troops almost at will, which in turn, it suggested, led to the lack of discipline which followed. It went on to blame the Australians in part.

*Major-General Gordon Bennett, commanding the AIF* [the Australian Imperial Force] *in Malaya, had reached the conclusion by 'the Thursday' (the 12th February) that Singapore could not hold out. I have reason to believe that Major-General Gordon Bennett took a very pessimistic view of the situation on the 8th February; nor was he the only senior member of the services who feared an early collapse.*

*Many stories are current of the bad examples set by some members of the AIF. These troops, as we all know, have done magnificently in offensive actions in many parts of the world, but the very character-istics which have carried them to success in such operations appear to make them totally unsuitable for fighting on the retreat, where strict discipline is such a vital consideration. It is with great reluc-tance that I pursue this question of the behaviour of some members of the AIF, but there is little likelihood that these notes will be helpful if they are not frank. There were desertions. Men seen in Singapore town on the 9th and 10th February were heard to boast that they had come 'Down the line' because they were fed up with been plastered.*

The First Lord of the Admiralty pointed out that the editor of the *Straits Times* 'had no axe to grind' nor was he 'giving play to any per-sonal grudges'.

When I read this, it was the first time I had ever heard the blame for the fall of Singapore put so directly at the feet of the Australians; it was a powerful read. No wonder Churchill or successive British governments didn't want an enquiry held into what had happened at Singapore and its subsequent capitulation. If these views and opinions had been proffered at the time, the damage it could have caused politically between Britain and Australia could have been insurmountable.

The report continued on with the same Aussie-bashing theme:

> *When the SS* **Empire Star** *arrived at Batavia on the 14th February, several Australian deserters were taken ashore under armed guard.*
>
> *There have been allegations that those who fought valiantly in North Johore during the daylight hours, walked back to a nearby township at night to buy beer! There were cases of looting and rape. Inche Onn bin Jaafar, a member of the Johore State Council, who has always been very outspoken, but not disloyal to the British connection, made the accusation openly at a meeting of the council held in Johore Bahru about a week before I left Singapore. He alleged that British and Indian troops were not entirely blameless, but he was particularly scathing in his references to the Australians. He offered the council 'incontrovertible proof' of his charges and, after Inche Onn's opening remarks, the President arranged that the matter should be discussed in secret at a later stage. One of my reporters was present at this meeting and took a full note of the statements made. He also brought me a message from the Prime Minister of Johore (Ungku Aziz), who is a close personal friend, asking me if I would do my utmost to see that no mention of this matter was made public. Just one more example: A man came into my office about the 5th February to discuss a business matter. He produced a large cigarette case (gold). I asked him jokingly if he had won a big sweep at the last race meeting. He replied: 'No, 50 dollars from an Australian soldier, and no questions asked.' After I had expressed myself forcibly on his participation in such a transaction, he added, 'Well, the owner had lost it anyway, and if I hadn't bought it somebody else would.*

The report continued, this time talking about the Indian troops and the part that they had played in the debacle, in essence claiming that some of them had been persuaded by pamphlets dropped by Japanese aircraft to surrender, with the promise that if they did, they would go unharmed. The report states there is evidence that the Japanese promise was kept when Indian troops did in fact surrender. They were even offered the opportunity to join the Japanese forces and fight with them against the British. The pamphlet claimed that Indian troops were being placed in the front line while white British troops were being held in the background.

The report praised the British troops, in particular the Argyles, the East Surreys and the Leicesters, along with the Gordons. The Loyals were described as being adequate. They were sent into the fight within seventy-two hours of their arrival and most if not all had had no fighting experience.

The issue of equipment was then covered. It claimed that Allied forces were not lacking equipment, if anything they had too much for the environment in which they were fighting. In comparison, the Japanese soldiers were lightly dressed and equipped. Their chosen modes of transport were either on foot or by bicycle, which allowed them to be flexible in their tactics and cover large distances in relatively short periods of time. It was claimed that Allied troops were not able to counter the infiltration tactics of the Japanese and were too strongly dependent on motorised transport to move them about, rather than old-fashioned marching. The only British troops to escape this criticism were the Argyll and Sutherland Highlanders, who at one stage of the retreat through Malaya covered 100 miles from Mersing to Singapore, highlighting the point that they were mobile as men as well as in a unit formation.

Then the report moved on to the Malays. Its first description of them was as follows:

> *Actually the Malays as a whole did very little to help either side. There were a few active traitors among them, but for the most part their one idea was to keep themselves out of trouble. They willingly sold bicycles for 'Malayan money' printed in Japan, and they were easily persuaded to give information regarding jungle paths and the routes taken by our troops. Among the tricks of active traitors were the laying of large cardboard arrows to direct aircraft to buildings occupied as Headquarters, marking trees to show the locality of gun positions and troop concentrations.*

My chapter on Lieutenant Adnan bin Saidi of the Royal Malay Regiment, and his two brothers who also fought in the war, doesn't suggest that the last statement in the report applied to a large number of brave and heroic Malayans, who willingly fought and died fighting the Japanese.

The report also highlighted the lack of coordinated civilian defences, with nobody apparently having overall control or, as it also appeared, wanting to take that responsibility. It didn't seem that this aspect of the defence of the island had been given too much thought. There was certainly no pre-planned, tried and trusted policy in place to deal with such an eventuality.

The last paragraph of the report read as follows:

> *Singapore fell so rapidly because the fight for it was less than half hearted; and for that fact, lack of inspiring leadership must be held largely responsible. Cables have spoken of 73,000 Services prisoners. Let us be conservative and put the total at 60,000. The original Japanese landing on the island was made in the sector held by the Australians. About 5,000 men gained a footing on the first night. A counter attack on the following day was a failure and on the second night the enemy strengthened his hold. From the moment that a garrison of at least 60,000 failed to repel an invading force of 5,000, the battle for Singapore was lost.*

What was intriguing about this report was the fact that not once did it lay any blame for the failings at Singapore at the feet of Winston Churchill, nor any other politician for that matter, regardless of their political persuasion.

There has always been some disagreement over the number of soldiers the Japanese had when they invaded Singapore, most historians suggesting the figure was in the region of 30,000. It is therefore worth noting that when Japan surrendered Singapore back to the British in September 1945, more than 70,000 Japanese soldiers were taken in to captivity by the British.

# CHAPTER SIXTEEN

# THE DEFENCE OF SINGAPORE

There was a massive irony attached to the fall of Singapore in 1942, which was that the British had being seriously addressing the issue of the island's defences for five years, going back to 1937. The main reason for this was Japan's continued military actions in the region which culminated in the Second Sino-Japanese war with China, which began on 7 July 1937.

Senior military figures had advised the British government on more than one occasion that much more was needed to be done in the areas of physical defences, manpower and equipment; but they were not listened to by the politicians.

Major General William Dobbie had been appointed General Officer Commanding of the Malaya Command on 8 November 1935 and was stationed in Singapore. In 1936 he decided that a review of troop numbers in Malaya was needed in light of the potential threat of Japanese military involvement in the area. The person Dobbie chose to carry out this review was his chief staff officer, Arthur Percival, who would himself become General Officer Commanding Malaya in April 1941.

The main focus of the review was to consider the most likely location where Japanese forces might carry out an attack on Malaya. Percival's report, which was completed in late 1937, highlighted Northern Malaya as such a location. It also pointed out that for Singapore to remain secure, Malaya needed to be defended, because if the latter fell victim to Japanese aggression, then Singapore was almost certain to suffer the same fate.

In May 1938 Dobbie sent a letter to the chief of staff in London explaining that he believed that any attack on Singapore by the Japanese was going to come through Malaya and the most likely time for this would be during the monsoon season which took place between November and March.

They received one additional battalion for Malaya and £60,000 to improve defences in southern Malaya.

With the outbreak of the Second World War in Europe in 1939, the need to bolster Singapore's defensive capabilities was felt to be a priority by the heads of the Army, Navy and Air Force. To this end they sent a request to London asking for 566 aircraft. The answer from the chiefs of staff was that 336 aircraft was felt to be a sufficient number, but that they would take some time to deliver to the island. The chiefs of staff also felt that the number of soldiers in the region should be increased, and to this end their intention was to send an entire infantry division from India. The chiefs of staff hadn't reckoned on Winston Churchill, who wasn't agreeable to either an increase in the number of aircraft or manpower, although the 9th Indian Division did arrive in Singapore in April 1941.

Despite £60,000 having been allocated for the improvement of defensive installations in southern Malaya, immediately across the causeway from Singapore, no work of any major significance was ever carried out. The reality of the situation appeared to be that the only means of defending Singapore from a Japanese attack from Malaya was to blow up the causeway that connected the two land masses.

Having stated that he believed any attack on Singapore by the Japanese would come through Malaya, why Percival then did nothing to bolster the defences along the coastline of northern Singapore is a mystery.

The Orbis Publishing magazine *World War Two* notes the fact that by 1941 both Britain and America knew full well that Japan was already spending forty-nine per cent of her budgetary expenditure on armaments, which surely must have made both countries somewhat concerned as to what Japan's long term intentions were. Even up until the eve of the attack on Pearl Harbor some of the propaganda that the Allies were coming out with in relation to the Japanese was somewhat strange. For instance, one of the things claimed was:

> *According to some scientists it was a well-established fact that through a deficiency of vitamin C, the Japanese lacked acuity of vision; hence they would make poor air pilots and at sea would be no match for British and American sailors after sunset.*

As well as this, Captain Russell Grenfell, of British Military Intelligence, stated that 'Japanese aircraft and airmen were not worth half of their British counterparts.'

It wouldn't be long until the Allied nations would find out at first hand just how wrong they had been in so many of their preconceived ideas about the Japanese.

History does not reflect well on Percival and his actions in surrendering Singapore so readily to the Japanese, but it can be argued that this epitaph is not fair. The main criticism has always been that the larger British force of some 90,000 men surrendered to a much smaller Japanese force of 30,000. That is a fair point, especially as Winston Churchill had determined that there should be no surrender of Singapore and if necessary troops and officers alike should fight to the death. There was also the matter of Percival having some 6,000 Royal Engineers under his command, yet he chose not to erect any defences along the northern coastline of Singapore, and was quoted as saying, 'Defences are bad for morale.'

Some would say that Percival was simply no more than an unfortunate scapegoat, easily targeted to save the blushes of blundering politicians who continuously made the wrong decisions for political and not sound military reasons.

Winston Churchill on the other hand escaped largely unscathed by the entire affair, yet he had a lot to answer for in the eventual downfall of Singapore, the 'Worst disaster in British history' as he called it, though he was way off the mark as that still has to be the first day of the Battle of the Somme, 1 July 1916. He refused to send more troops to the island, although the 9th Indian Division were eventually sent despite his protestations. He sent 200 fewer aircraft than had been requested, stating that such large numbers were not warranted. Worst of all, he removed the 350 tanks which had been in Malaya and sent them to assist on the Russian Front, leaving Malaya and Singapore greatly weakened. The Japanese had about 200.

Attempts by the British Malaya Command to carry out Operation Matador were also ultimately thwarted by the British Government. This was a pre-emptive plan to send troops to the port city of Songkhla and Pattani in southern Thailand to prevent invading Japanese forces from landing in either location and utilising the nearby airports and seaports, from where they could then more readily invade both Malaya and Singapore.

The reality is that even if the operation had gone ahead and had been successful, the Japanese could have undoubtedly found alternative locations for their landings, but at least the British and their Commonwealth Allies would have been doing something positive and taking the initiative rather than just waiting around to see what the Japanese would do next.

After the surrender, Percival was initially held in Changi prison, which the Japanese used as a prisoner of war camp, but in August 1942 he was moved to Manchuria, where he remained in captivity until the end of the war, returning to England in September 1945. He retired from the Army the following year.

# CHAPTER SEVENTEEN

# VICTORIA CROSSES MALAYA/ SINGAPORE 1941–45

Between January 1941 and July 1945, six men were awarded the Victoria Cross for acts of gallantry during either the Malaya Campaign or the Battle of Singapore.

Their individual stories are told here in date order of the actions for which they were awarded.

**Arthur Edward Cumming** VC OBE MC was a Lieutenant Colonel with the 2nd/12th Battalion, Frontier Force Regiment, which was part of the Indian Army.

On 3 January 1942 near Kuantan, during the Battle of Malaya, Cumming and his men were defending an Allied airfield when they came under a heavy and sustained Japanese attack, during which their position was penetrated.

Part of the citation for Cumming's Victoria Cross was as follows:

> On 3 January 1942 near Kuantan, Malaya, the Japanese made a furious attack on the battalion and a strong enemy force penetrated the position. Lieutenant-Colonel Cumming, with a small party of men, immediately led a counter attack and although all of his men became casualties and he, himself, had two bayonet wounds in the stomach, he managed to restore the situation sufficiently for the major portion of the battalion and its vehicles to be withdrawn. Later he drove in a carrier, under heavy fire, collecting isolated detachments of his men and was again wounded. His gallant actions helped the brigade to withdraw safely.

Cummings was evacuated from Singapore before Percival surrendered the island to the Japanese. What would have become of him if he had remained on the island as a patient at the Alexandra Military Hospital can only be guessed.

**Charles Groves Wright Anderson** VC MC was an interesting character and a remarkable man.

He was born in Cape Town, South Africa, on 12 February 1897 to an English father and a Belgian mother. When he was 3 years of age the family up and moved to Nairobi in Kenya where his father took up farming. At the age of 10 Charles was sent by his parents to England to be educated.

At the outbreak of the First World War Anderson returned to Kenya and later joined the Calcutta Volunteer Battalion as a Gunner, but was commissioned as a lieutenant into the 3rd Battalion, Kings African Rifles, on 13 October 1916. He saw action in the East African campaign where he was awarded a Military Cross for his gallantry. He was demobbed in February 1919 and returned to Kenya and a life of farming. He emigrated to Australia in 1934, two years after marrying an Australian, Edith Tout.

In the period between the wars Anderson had been a part-time soldier and joined the Citizens Military Forces, or Army Reserve. At the beginning of the Second World War he joined the Second Australian Imperial Force and volunteered for overseas service. Under the terms of the Australian Defence Act 1903 no member of the Australian armed forces, whether they were part-time or full-time soldiers, could be made to serve abroad; anyone who did, had to volunteer.

In February 1941, Anderson, by now a major, was deployed to Malaya with the newly formed 2nd/19th Battalion, which was part of the 8th Division of the Australian Army. The last major battle of the Malaya campaign, before the Japanese poured in to Singapore, was the Battle of Maur which took place between 14 and 22 January 1942 and ended as a resounding success for Japanese forces under the command of General Takuma Nishimura, who would later be executed by the Australians on 11 June 1951 in connection with the Parit Sulong Massacre which took place at the end of the Battle of Muar. During the battle, Anderson and a group of men he was leading found themselves cut off and in Japanese-held territory. By now it was a race to reach the causeway and the safety of Singapore. The fifteen-mile journey from Muar to Parit Sulong wasn't without incident and more than once Anderson and his men were engaged in hand-to-hand fighting with Japanese forces, which also involved him leading his men in a bayonet charge.

At Parit Sulong, which was a small town in the Johore region of Malaya, Anderson and his men were once again surrounded by Japanese forces. The bridge they needed to cross to get through the town so as to be able to continue their journey on towards Yong Peng, where the intention was to meet up with the main Australian force before heading for the safety of Singapore, was blocked by a Japanese machine gun unit. Fierce fighting ensued for several days with Anderson's men sustaining heavy casualties to a larger Japanese force who were holding their position and refusing to surrender.

Despite Anderson's best efforts to have his wounded evacuated so that they could be treated, the Japanese refused to cooperate and would not let them leave the area of the fighting. Soon afterwards Anderson took the decision to relinquish his position and instruct all of his able-bodied men to escape the best way they could through the jungle and make their way to Yong Peng, leaving behind 150 Australian and Indian wounded in the belief that they would be cared for by the Japanese. Sadly every single one of them was murdered on their capture in what became known as the Parit Sulong massacre, which I have covered in more detail in another chapter.

For his actions and leadership over the four days between 18 and 22 January 1942, Anderson was awarded the Victoria Cross.

The citation for the award of his Victoria Cross was listed in the *London Gazette* on 13 February 1942. It read as follows:

> *For setting a magnificent example of brave leadership, determination and outstanding courage. He not only showed fighting qualities of the very highest order, but throughout exposed himself to danger without any regard for his own personal safety.*

Anderson made it back to Singapore. By 13 February 1942, out of an original complement of 900, the men of the 2nd/19th Battalion were down to just 180. Anderson was one of the Commonwealth soldiers who was taken prisoner by the Japanese once Percival had officially surrendered, and spent the remainder of the war in captivity. He was repatriated at the end of the war and returned to Australia. He died on 11 November 1988 at the age of 91.

**Arthur Stewart King Scarf** VC was a squadron leader with No. 62 Squadron and was based at Alor Star on the west coast of Malaya close to the border with Thailand. On 9 December 1941, just as the Japanese Navy was attacking the American Fleet at Pearl Harbor, the Japanese Army was landing at Singora as it began its invasion of Thailand.

Scarf and his colleagues at No. 62 Squadron were ordered to make a daylight raid on Singora, to try to stop the Japanese Air Force who were stationed there from effectively supporting their ground troops as they began landing in Thailand.

For his actions that day, Scarf was awarded the Victoria Cross. The citation for his award was only published in the *London Gazette* on 21 June 1946:

> *The King has been graciously pleased to confer the posthumous award of the Victoria Cross to the undermentioned Officer in recognition of most conspicuous bravery:-*

*Squadron Leader Arthur Stewart King Scarf (37693) Royal Air Force, No. 62 Squadron.*

*On 9th December 1941, all available aircraft from the Royal Air Force Station, Butterworth, Malaya, were ordered to make a daylight attack on the advanced operational base of the Japanese Air Force at Singora, Thailand. From this base the enemy fighter squadrons were supporting the landing operations.*

*The aircraft detailed for the sortie were on the point of taking off when the enemy made a combined dive bombing and low level machine gun attack on the airfield. All our aircraft were destroyed or damaged with the exception of the Blenheim piloted by Squadron Leader Scarf. This aircraft had become airborne a few seconds before the attack started.*

*Squadron Leader Scarf circled the airfield and witnessed the disaster. It would have been reasonable had he abandoned the projected operation which was intended to be a formation sortie. He decided, however, to press on to Singora in his single aircraft. Although he knew this individual action could not inflict much material damage on the enemy, he nevertheless appreciated the moral effect which it would have on the remainder of the squadron, who were helplessly watching their aircraft burning on the ground.*

*Squadron Leader Scarf completed his attack successfully. The opposition over the target was severe and included attacks by a considerable number of enemy fighters. In the course of these encounters Squadron Leader Scarf was mortally wounded.*

*The enemy continued to engage him in a running fight, which lasted until he had regained the Malayan border. Squadron Leader Scarf fought a brilliant evasive action in a valiant attempt to return to his base. Although he displayed the utmost gallantry and determination, he was, owing to his wounds, unable to accomplish this. He made a successful forced landing at Alor Star without causing any injury to his crew. He was received into hospital as soon as possible, but died shortly after admission.*

*Squadron Leader Scarf displayed supreme heroism in the face of tremendous odds and his splendid example of self-sacrifice will long be remembered.*

Scarf's other crew that fateful day were Sergeant, later Squadron Leader, Paddy Calder, who was awarded the Distinguished Flying Medal for his actions during the same operation, and Sergeant Cyril Rich, who was subsequently killed in action in 1943, was posthumously mentioned in despatches.

Percival arriving in Singapore in April 1941 as General Officer Commanding Malaya.

Australian soldiers fighting a rearguard action during the retreat from Malaya.

Raffles hotel, November 1941.

Battle Box entrance. (Courtesy of Singapore History Consultants at Battle Box)

Guard duty at Battle Box entrance. (Courtesy of Singapore History Consultants at Battle Box)

Battle Box, a guard showing the way. (Courtesy of Singapore History Consultants at Battle Box)

Battle Box telephone room. (Courtesy of Singapore History Consultants at Battle Box)

Intel room inside the Battle Box. (Courtesy of Singapore History Consultants at Battle Box)

Battle Box operations room before the surrender of Singapore. (Courtesy of Singapore History Consultants at Battle Box)

Member of Percival's staff in the Battle Box. (Courtesy of Singapore History Consultants at Battle Box)

Percival in his office in the Battle Box. (Courtesy of Singapore History Consultants at Battle Box)

The fateful meeting that determined the surrender of Singapore. (Courtesy of Singapore History Consultants at Battle Box)

British troops surrendering to Japanese troops in Singapore.

Japanese soldiers march triumphantly into Singapore city.

Percival and staff officers on route to surrender to the Japanese on 15 February 1942.

Percival and colleagues on their way to surrender, 15 February 1942.

Percival about to sign the surrender document handing Singapore over to the Japanese. 15 February 1942.

Sister Vivian Bullwinkel who survived the massacre at Bangka Island.

MV *Krait* used as part of Operation Jaywick, 27 September 1943.
(Courtesy of Mrs Wynn Robinson)

Lieutenant Adnan Saidi.

Lim Bo Seng.

Lim Bo Seng's funeral in Singapore, 15 February 1942.

Malay Sailor on guard
at Singapore Naval Base.

Memorial to Lim Bo Seng,
in Singapore.

Japanese soldiers in Singapore.

Japanese soldiers relaxing in Singapore.

Japanese surrender of Singapore ceremony, at the Old Supreme Court Building, 12 September 1945.

Signing by General Douglas MacArthur on board USS *Missouri* on 2 September 1945.

Japanese surrendering at Singapore on 12 September 1945.

Commonwealth and Japanese officers leaving the surrender ceremony, 12 September 1945.

Japanese prisoners of war working on the Padang, which sits opposite the Old Supreme Court Building in Singapore.

Singapore City. Old Supreme Court House can be seen in the top right of photograph.

Changi prison after the Japanese surrender, September 1945.

Australian PoWs liberated after Japanese had surrendered Singapore to the Allies.

Civilian War
Memorial, Singapore.
(Courtesy of Aron Manzanillo)

Kranji War Cemetery,
Singapore.

**Thomas Wilkinson** VC was a temporary lieutenant in the Royal Naval Reserve and the commander of HMS *Li Wo*, a patrol vessel which had previously been a passenger steamer. Since having left Singapore on 13 February 1942, she had fought off four aerial attacks from a total of fifty-two Japanese aircraft, which had left her with considerable damage.

On 14 February 1942 the *Li Wo* was in the Java Sea just off the coast of Malaya, sailing between Singapore and Batavia when Wilkinson sighted two enemy convoys, one of which was being escorted by Japanese naval vessels.

Despite the odds of success being extremely low and death being the most likely outcome, Wilkinson informed his crew that not only had he decided to attack one of the convoys but that he intended to fight to the last in an effort to inflict some damage on the passing convoy. Wilkinson's entire crew, fully aware of the likely outcome of such an attack against a bigger, faster and more powerful enemy, were all in agreement with his intentions.

They attacked and set fire to a Japanese transporter which because of the damage Wilkinson and his crew inflicted on her subsequently had to be abandoned. Not satisfied with what they had achieved they continued their attack and engaged a Japanese heavy cruiser which as part of its armoury had eight-inch guns on its deck which were capable of causing extensive damage to anything they hit. The ships engaged each other for over an hour, each trying to outmanoeuvre the other while at the same time trying to stay afloat, before the *Li Woo* was struck at point blank range.

Wilkinson gave the order for his crew to abandon ship while he stayed on board and went down with it. Out of eighty-four men on board only seven survived, all of whom were taken prisoner by the Japanese.

From this one action ten other crew of the *Li Wo* received gallantry awards for their actions. Six were mentioned in despatches, three of whom were posthumously given awards. There were two awards of the Distinguished Service Medal, one of the Distinguished Service Order and one of the Conspicuous Gallantry Medal. Collectively, the awards made HMS *Li Wo* the most decorated small ship in the Royal Navy during the course of the Second World War.

**Ian Edward Fraser** VC DSO RD and Bar joined the Royal Navy in 1939. In 1943, when only 23 years of age, he was awarded the Distinguished Service Cross for his 'bravery and skill in successful submarine patrols' while serving on the British Naval submarine HMS *Sahib*.

He became a lieutenant in the Royal Naval Reserve a year later in 1944 and served on HMS *Bonaventure* from 7 November 1944 until the end of the war. The *Bonaventure* was a depot ship for X class midget submarines.

The citation for the award of his Victoria Cross was published in the *London Gazette* dated 13 November 1945 and read as follows:

> *Whitehall, 13th November 1945.*
>
> *The King has been graciously pleased to approve the award of the Victoria Cross for valour:-*
>
> *Lieutenant Ian Edward FRASER, DSC, RNR.*
>
> *Lieutenant Fraser commanded His Majesty's Midget Submarine XE-3 in a successful attack on a Japanese heavy cruiser of the Atago class at her moorings in Johore Strait, Singapore, on 31st July 1945. During the long approach up the Singapore Straits, XE-3 deliberately left the believed safe channel and entered mined waters to avoid suspected hydrophone posts. The target was aground, or nearly aground, both fore and aft, and only under the midships portion was there sufficient water for XE-3 to place herself under the cruiser. For forty minutes XE-3 pushed her way along the seabed until finally Lieutenant Fraser managed to force her right under the centre of the cruiser. Here he placed the limpets and dropped his main side charge. Great difficulty was experienced in extricating the craft after the attack had been completed, but finally XE-3 was clear, and commenced her long return journey out to sea. The courage and determination of Lieutenant Fraser are beyond all praise. Any man not possessed of relentless determination to achieve his object in full, regardless of all consequences, would have dropped his charge alongside the target instead of persisting until he had forced his submarine right under the cruiser. The approach and withdrawal entailed a passage of 80 miles through water which had been mined by both the enemy and ourselves, past hydrophone positions, over loops and controlled minefields, and through an anti-submarine boom.*

Fraser left the Royal Navy in 1947 and, realizing that frogman type diving was the way forward, having many advantages over what had been the older standard type diving suits, set up his own commercial diving company. He died on 1 September 2008 aged 87 at Arrowe Park Hospital, Merseyside.

**James Joseph Magennis** (originally spelt McGinnes) VC was born in Belfast on 27 October 1919. He joined the Royal Navy on 3 June 1935 when he enlisted as a 15-year-old boy seaman. Over the next seven years he served on numerous different British warships before joining the submarine branch in December 1942. In March 1943 he volunteered for what was entitled 'Special and hazardous duties', namely working on midget submarines, or X craft as they were also referred to, which had only come into service that year. But first he had to train and qualify as a diver.

The first use of this newly developed midget submarine was in Operation Source, in which Magennis was involved. The German battleship *Tirpitz* was holed up in the harbour of the Norwegian village of Kafjord when two British midget submarines, HMS *X6* and HMS *X7*, managed to penetrate the harbour's defences before attaching mines to the hull of the ship, which along with bombs dropped by the RAF helped to disable the *Tirpitz*.

For his actions in the raid, Magennis was mentioned in despatches 'for his bravery and devotion to duty'.

Magennis was one of the four-man crew of the British midget submarine HMS *XE3* which had been tasked with sinking the Japanese cruiser *Takao*, which was moored in the Straits of Johore off of Singapore. HMS *XE3* was towed into the Straits of Johore by the British submarine *Stygian*, but still had to undertake a journey of some forty miles, travelling through minefields and hydrophone listening posts to reach her intended target, a journey which would take nearly fourteen hours to complete.

Once in position Magennis, the crew's designated diver, spent more than half an hour chipping away at barnacles on the hull of the *Takao* before he could attach the limpet mines, all the time hoping and praying that the noise he was making wouldn't be picked up from inside the ship. His task finished, he returned to the midget submarine. Just as *XE3* was to begin her homeward-bound journey Lieutenant Fraser realized there was a problem with one of the limpets. Magennis volunteered to go and deal with it. After several minutes of strenuous effort he returned to the midget submarine, having successfully resolved the problem, allowing the crew to make good their escape to their pickup point with the *Stygian*.

The citation for Magennis's award of the Victoria Cross appeared in the *London Gazette* dated 13 November 1945 and read as follows:

> *Admiralty, Whitehall, 13th November, 1945.*
>
> *The King has been graciously pleased to approve the award of the Victoria Cross for valour to:-*
>
> *Temporary Acting Leading Seaman James Joseph Magennis, D/JX 144907.*

*Leading Seaman Magennis served as a diver in His Majesty's Midget Submarine XE-3 for her attack on 31 July 1945, on a Japanese cruiser of the Atago class. The diver's hatch could not be fully opened because XE-3 was tightly jammed under the target, and Magennis had to squeeze himself through the narrow space available.*

*He had experienced great difficulty in placing his limpets on the bottom of the cruiser owing both to the foul state of the bottom and to the pronounced slope upon which the limpets would not hold. Before a limpet could be placed therefore, Magennis had thoroughly to scrape the area clear of barnacles, and in order to secure the limpets he had to tie them in pairs by a line passing under the cruiser keel. This was very tiring work for a diver, and he was moreover handicapped by a steady leakage of oxygen which was ascending bubbles to the surface. A lesser man would have been content to place a few limpets and then return to the craft. Magennis, however, persisted until he had placed his full outfit before returning to the craft in an exhausted condition. Shortly after withdrawing Lieutenant Fraser endeavoured to jettison his limpet carriers, but one of these would not release itself and fall clear of the craft. Despite his exhaustion, his oxygen leak and the fact that there was every probability of his being sighted, Magennis at once volunteered to leave the craft and free the carrier rather than allow a less experienced diver to undertake the job. After seven minutes of nerve racking work he succeeded in releasing the carrier. Magennis displayed very great courage and devotion to duty and complete disregard for his own safety.*

It transpired that HMS *XE1*, which was part of the same operation but was supposed to be placing its limpet mines on another Japanese vessel close by, ended up placing them on the hull of the *Takao* as well. All eight men from the two midget submarines received gallantry awards for their individual actions during the operation.

Besides Fraser and Magennis the following men also received awards: the other two members of Fraser and Magennis's crew, Sub-Lieutenant William James Lanyon Smith received the Distinguished Service Cross and Engine Room Artificer Third Class Charles Alfred Reed received the Conspicuous Gallantry Medal. The following four crew members of HMS *XE1* received awards: Lieutenant John Elliot Smart and Sub-Lieutenant Harold Edwin Harper were both awarded the Distinguished Service Cross, and Engine Room Artificer Fourth Class Henry James Fishleigh and Leading Seaman Walter Henry

Arthur Pomeroy received the Distinguished Service Medal for their individual acts of bravery.

Magennis was the only recipient of the Victoria Cross from Northern Ireland during the Second World War. He was married in 1946 to Edith Skidmore and they went on to have four sons. He stayed in the Navy after the war before finally leaving in 1949. He died on 11 February 1986 aged 67.

# CHAPTER EIGHTEEN

# LIM BO SENG

Lim Bo Seng was born in Meilin Town in the province of Fujian, which is situated on the southeast coast of China. Lim was the eleventh child but only son of a building constructor, Lim Loh, which meant that his family were reasonably well off. Because of this they could afford to send a 16-year-old Lim Bo Seng to Singapore in 1925 to study at the prestigious Raffles Institution. The school had been founded on 5 June 1823 by Sir Stamford Raffles to provide education for the sons of employees of the British East India Company and the children of local community leaders. After leaving there, Lim went on to study business at the University of Hong Kong.

In 1930, at the age of 21, he married Gan Choo Neo and they went on to have eight children. By now he had inherited his father's construction company when he had died the previous year. He also had business interests in the manufacturing of bricks and the production of biscuits.

Besides being a successful businessman, Lim Bo Seng was also a prominent member of the Chinese community in Singapore, holding numerous positions of note including chairman of the Singapore Building Industry.

In 1937, the Second Sino-Japanese war broke out between China and Japan and although he had lived in Singapore for many years, Lim had never forgotten his roots. He became involved in fundraising events to help support China's war efforts as well as being a leading light in the boycotting of Japanese goods throughout Singapore.

In neighbouring Malaya there is a district called Dungun which is in the state of Terengganu. Prior to the Second World War, Japan owned an extremely profitable tin mine in Dungun, but relied heavily on Chinese workers for its labour force to excavate the tin so that it could be shipped back to Japan and used to make weapons for its military, some of which were in turn used in the fight against Chinese troops in the Sino-Japanese war. In February 1938, along with a colleague, Zhuang Huiguan, Lim went to the tin mine in Dungun to try to persuade the workers to go on strike. It was a big ask, because despite their own personal feelings about mining the tin for their Japanese masters, they needed to work to be able to feed their families. They didn't manage to get all of the workers to go on strike but some of the workers not only stopped working at the tin mine but returned with Lim and Zhuang Huiguan to Singapore. Those he persuaded to go on strike and leave the mine, he found work for within the Singaporean community. Lim was also involved in the boycotting of Japanese goods and fundraising to support China's war effort.

As the threat of Japanese imperialism gradually increased throughout South East Asia, so the realization grew that both Malaya and Singapore could also be on Japan's list of places to invade. To help combat this growing threat there was an increase in the number of young Malayan and Singaporean men joining local units such as the Malay Regiment, the Malayan Naval Volunteer Reserve, the Straits Settlements Volunteer Force, and its Reserve. In December 1941, Lim was put in charge of the Straits Settlements Volunteer Force which he organised to help defend the island. Members of the Volunteer Force fought bravely and tenaciously against the Japanese during the Battle of Singapore only to then become prisoners of war when the British surrendered Singapore on 15 February 1942.

Just before the invasion of Singapore, Lim left for Indonesia and travelled on to India. He ended up in Chungking, China, where he helped set up and train a network of spies to carry out missions that were anti-Japanese. There he teamed up with Captain John Davis of the British Army's Special Operations Executive which was the forerunner of the Special Air Service, the SAS. With him he set up 'Force 136' which was a Sino-British guerrilla unit. Together they recruited and trained hundreds of young Chinese and Indian men to carry out intelligence gathering missions against the Japanese. Operation Gustavus was about setting up a spy network throughout Malaya and Singapore to gain intelligence about Japanese activities, movements and numbers of military personnel and equipment at their disposal.

As the commanding officer of the Malayan Chinese section of Force 136, Lim Bo Seng was dropped off by the Dutch submarine *O 23* at Bagan Datoh in Perak on 2 November 1943 with the intention of joining up with British and Chinese officers who were already in the area working with anti-Japanese forces.

In January 1944 the Japanese captured a communist guerrilla fighter who under interrogation revealed the details of an Allied spy network that was operating in the area. The Japanese quickly launched a full-scale counter-espionage operation to capture as many people who were involved in the network as possible. On 24 March, a local fisherman by the name of Chua Koon Eng was arrested by the Kempeitai. He informed his captors that he had been approached by members of Force 136 requesting the use of his fishing boat for their work in the area. Within a week the entire spy network had been uncovered and destroyed.

On 23 March 1944, while in the town of Gopeng, Lim Bo Seng was stopped at a Japanese roadblock and arrested. Under interrogation and torture he revealed nothing about his activities or that of Force 136. Whether the Japanese realized who they had detained is not clear as Lim often used a false name when travelling about.

While being held prisoner at Batu Gajah prison, Lim contracted dysentery and quickly started to deteriorate. He died on 29 June 1944 and was buried in the grounds of the prison in an unmarked grave.

After Japan's surrender Lim's remains were recovered and brought back to Singapore on 7 December 1945. They were met at Tanjong Pagar railway station by a large crowd which included British Army officers and local businessmen. Lim's funeral service took place on 13 January 1946 at the City Hall after which he was buried at MacRitchie Reservoir with full military honours.

The Nationalist Government of the Republic of China posthumously awarded Lim the rank of Major General.

Lim Bo Seng's memorial was unveiled on 29 June 1954, on the tenth anniversary of his death at Batu Gajah prison. It was unveiled by Sir Charles Loewen, who at the time was commander-in-chief of the Far East Land Forces.

The cost of the memorial was funded by donations from the Chinese community in Singapore and the land on which the memorial stands was donated by the Singapore government.

# CHAPTER NINETEEN

# ELIZABETH CHOY – SINGAPORE WAR HEROINE

Elizabeth Choy, whose birth name was Yong Su-Moi, was born in Sabah, North Borneo on 29 November 1910, the eldest of eleven children. Her father was a civil servant who spent a lot of time moving around with his work. For her actions in Singapore during the Japanese occupation of the island between 1942 and 1945, she was considered by the people of Singapore to be a heroine.

While she was studying at St Monica's Boarding School in Sandakan, which is the second largest town in Sabah, she changed her Christian name from Su-Moi and adopted the English name of Elizabeth, which at the time was a normal thing for some young girls to do.

Elizabeth wanted to continue her higher education when she moved to Singapore, but with ten other siblings to look after as well as Elizabeth her parents could not afford to pay for her tuition fees. She had no option but to find herself a job to save money to pay the fees herself. She started teaching at different schools and was eventually able to realize her dream and attend the prestigious Raffles College, which later became the National University of Singapore.

During the war years, she more than did her bit for her adopted country. When the Japanese invaded Malaya, Elizabeth became a second lieutenant in the women's auxiliary wing of the Singapore Volunteer Reserves, which was also known as the Singapore Special Constabulary. This was a militia unit, first established way back in 1854.

As if her work as a second lieutenant didn't keep her busy enough, she was also a volunteer nurse with the Medical Auxiliary Service. When Singapore fell to the Japanese in February 1942, Elizabeth and her husband, Choy Khun Heng, whom she had married in August 1941, set up a canteen at the Tan Tock Seng Hospital, after all of the doctors and patients had been moved there from the Miyako Hospital.

Without the Japanese knowing, they managed to help many prisoners of war and civilian internees who were being held at Changi prison, by getting them cash, clothing, medicines and long-awaited letters from their loved ones.

In what became known as the Double Tenth Incident, when in Singapore Harbour six Japanese ships were sunk in an audacious raid that was carried out by Australian and British members of the 'Z' Special Unit, which I have written about in a previous chapter in the book, Elizabeth and her husband were two of the civilians who were arrested on suspicion of being involved in organising the raid. This came about after an informant told the Kempeitai that Choy Khun Heng, Elizabeth's husband, was responsible for smuggling money to some of those who were being held at Changi prison. Elizabeth knew that her husband had been detained by the Kempeitai, but as the days went by and she had not heard anything from them, she took the decision to go to their East District Branch office, which was also the headquarters of the Kempeitai in Singapore. It was located at the Young Men's Christian Association (YMCA) building on Stamford Road.

To everyday civilians it was not somewhere they wanted to end up, because this is where the Kempeitai carried out their interrogation of suspects, which could quite easily turn into torture if the questions they asked didn't illicit the answers they wanted.

The Kempeitai had determined that those individuals who they arrested had to prove their innocence, rather than them having to prove that they were guilty. The torture techniques which they employed were officially known to the Kempeitai as 'treatments'. Some of the techniques which they used were described by witnesses at the subsequent war crimes trials.

- **Eardrum piercing:** The pointed end of a pencil was placed in to a victim's ear until it pierced the eardrum.
- **Water torture:** The victim was tied up and laid flat out on the floor. Water was then pushed into their body through their nose and mouth, causing their stomach to become bloated. The interrogators would then jump on the victim's stomach to force the water out. They would continue this process until the victim passed out.
- **The tearing out of finger and toe nails:** The Kempeitai would stick toothpicks under the nails, then rip the nails out with the use of pliers.
- **Beatings:** The victims were beaten with a combination of different implements which included bamboo or wooden sticks, whips, belt buckles, metal bars, or the butt of a revolver.
- **Burning or electric shocks:** Victims had the sensitive parts of their anatomy burnt with candles, lighted cigarettes, boiling water or oil, or live electric wires.

These were just some of the torture techniques used by the Kempeitai. After victims had been tortured, dependent on what they had confessed to, they would either be imprisoned or, in some cases, they would be executed. After Singapore fell to the Japanese, anybody who was arrested by the Kempeitai for looting was beheaded and their heads placed on spikes outside their headquarters as a deterrent to others.

Back to Elizabeth: The Kempeitai denied any knowledge of having ever arrested her husband. Three weeks later she was asked to return to the Kempeitai's headquarters, which she did, possibly in the belief that she was going to be told something about her husband, but she wasn't. Instead they arrested her and placed her in one of their cells. She was one of those who the Kempeitai tortured.

At the war crimes trials which took place in Singapore after the war, another internee who was a witness at one of the trials said that he had seen Elizabeth Choy stripped of her clothes and severely beaten by Kempeitai officers.

Thankfully Elizabeth survived her ordeal at the hands of the Kempeitai and when the Japanese surrendered she was released from her captivity. The heroic acts which she carried out, along with her husband, during the occupation by helping others who had been interned by the Japanese, often at great risk to herself, had not gone unnoticed.

Elizabeth was invited by Lady Mountbatten to attend the official Japanese surrender ceremony that took place at City Hall, Singapore, on 12 September 1945. Her escorts for the day were Sir Shenton Thomas, the Governor of Singapore, and his wife, to whom Elizabeth had sent medicines while they were interned at Changi prison.

The Choys were invited to go and stay in England after the war to help with their recuperation. They ended up staying there for four years during which time they were both awarded the OBE for what they had done in assisting British prisoners of war and civilian internees who had been held in Malaya and Singapore during the three-year Japanese occupation of the region.

On her return to Singapore in 1949 she did many things and was given many awards, but teaching was her main choice of work; she worked at St Andrews School in Singapore until 1973. She also dabbled in politics for a few years, eventually retiring from that in the mid-1950s. She died on 14 September 2006 at the age of 95.

# CHAPTER TWENTY

# OPERATION RIMAU

The 'Z' Special Unit was a combination of the British Army's Special Operations Executive (SOE), the forerunner of the Special Air Service (SAS), and Special Operations Australia (SOA). They were also known as the Services Reconnaissance Department (SRD). Although a joint adventure, the majority of its men were in fact Australian; besides the British, there were also men from Holland, New Zealand, Timor and Indonesia.

The unit, formed in March 1942, was based in Melbourne in Australia. Its remit would be to operate behind Japanese lines throughout South East Asia, with its main purposes being that of reconnaissance to gather intelligence and sabotage as a part of a campaign of guerrilla warfare. During its four-year existence it carried out a total of eighty-one covert operations throughout the South West Pacific. In most cases its operatives would either be inserted into its location by a parachute jump or by submarine.

As is shown in an earlier chapter of the book, Operation Jaywick was one of its successes. Operation Rimau (Rimau is the Malay word for Tiger) on the other hand is an example of just how a similarly meticulously planned operation could go so badly wrong, not because of poor planning but because of nothing more sinister than chance.

Six members of the Operation Rimau team were veterans of the Operation Jaywick operation, so it was a highly experienced team. Once again the plan was to attack Japanese shipping inside Keppel Harbour in Singapore. This time they were to use fifteen one-man, motorised, submersible canoes, known as Sleeping Beauties, to make their attacks after which time the craft would all be scuttled. The men would then make good their escape in folding kayaks known as Folboats.

The operation, under the leadership of Colonel Ivan Lyon, began on the evening of 11 September 1944 when the unit left Freemantle in Australia on board the submarine HMS *Porpoise* before arriving at Pulau Merapas on 23 September.

Lyon's plan consisted of him and his team being self-sufficient for three months on the tiny island of Merapas which is off the east coast of Pulau Bintan. The location had been selected as it was believed to be uninhabited, but a periscope reconnaissance the next day spotted three men, believed to be local fishermen, next to a canoe on the beach. Having already dropped off the supplies, Lyon faced something of a quandary. He decided to change his plans. He left only one man, Lieutenant Walter Carey, on the island to look after the supplies. The same evening, 24 September, Lyon and the rest of his team then re-embarked in HMS *Porpoise* for the next part of the operation which was to find a local boat which could be used for the final part of the operation.

Four days later, on the afternoon of 28 September, they came across a junk, the *Mustika*, sailing off of the west coast of Borneo. It was boarded by members of Lyon's team.

Over the course of the evenings of 29 and 30 September 1944, the submersibles, the folboats, and other required stores for Lyon's missions were transferred form HMS *Porpoise* to the *Mustika*, close to the area of Pulau Pejantan. Once this had been completed, Major Walter Chapman and the Malayan crew remained on board HMS *Porpoise* and returned to Australia, while the newly acquired *Mustika* made her way back to the area of Merapas, where Lyon then dropped off three more members of his team to assist Carey with looking after the supplies.

On the day of the planned attack on Japanese shipping in Singapore harbour, 10 October 1944, fate stepped in and decided to take a part. There is some confusion as to what exactly happened, but the *Mustika* became embroiled with another vessel and shots were exchanged. There are differing reports that it was either a Japanese patrol boat or a Malayan police vessel; either way four of her crew were killed and one escaped. Lyon scuttled the *Mustika* and the Sleeping Beauties, then ordered most of his men to paddle their way back to Merapas in the folboats, while he and six other members of the team, Davison, Ross, Huston, Stewart, Campbell and Warne, made their way into the harbour at Singapore, where they set their limpet mines, which resulted in the sinking of three Japanese ships.

The main party had made it safely back to Merapas, but the six-man raiding party were not to fare so well. The Japanese caught up with Lyon and his team on 16 October on Soreh Island and during the ensuing gun battle Davison and Campbell were wounded. Lyon, Ross and Stewart fought a rearguard action so that the other four could escape. Lyon and Ross were killed by a Japanese grenade and Stewart was captured.

Davison and Campbell made their way to the island of Tapai by folboat where they both died on 18 October 1944; whether that was from their wounds or by swallowing their suicide pills is not clear. Huston and Warne both made it to Merapas.

Ten members of the team were captured and brought back to Singapore where they were held at Outram Road prison. The Japanese authorities put them on trial for espionage as they were not in military uniform at the time of their capture. They were all found guilty and sentenced to death. They were all beheaded on 7 July 1945, just a month before the Japanese would ultimately surrender to the Allies. Along with Lyon and four others, all ten of them were buried at Kranji War Cemetery. The ten men who were beheaded are as follows:

Walter George **Carey** was a lieutenant in the Australian Infantry, attached to 'Z' Special Unit. He was 31 years of age and his parents lived in Abbotsford, New South Wales, Australia.

Walter Gordon **Falls** DSM was an able seaman (S6543) in the Royal Australian Naval Reserve, attached to the 'Z' Special Unit. He was 25 years of age. His widow Joan lived at Casino, New South Wales.

Roland Bernard **Fletcher** was a corporal (NX80005) in the Australian Infantry, attached to 'Z' Special Unit. He was 29 years of age. Even though he was in the Australian Army, his parents lived at Canton, Cardiff, Wales.

David Peter **Gooley** was a sergeant (VX109893) in the Australian Infantry, attached to the 'Z' Special Unit. He was 27 years of age. His parents, David and Alice Ellen Gooley, lived at Caulfield, Victoria, Australia.

John Thomas **Hardy** was a lance corporal (NX140476) in the Australian Infantry, attached to the 'Z' Special Unit. He was 23 years of age. His parents lived in Lakemba, New South Wales.

Reginald Middleton **Ingleton** was 29 years of age and a major in the Royal Marines, attached to the 'Z' Special Unit. His widow Sybil lived in Wanstead, London.

Robert Charles **Page** DSO was a captain (NX19158) in the Australian Infantry, attached to the 'Z' Special Unit. He was 24 years of age. His widow, Roma Adelene Page, lived at Queanbeyan, Australian Capital Territory.

Albert Leslie **Sargant** was a lieutenant (VX15290) in the Australian Infantry, attached to the 'Z' Special Unit. He was 26 years of age. His widow Norma lived at Northbridge, New South Wales.

Clair Mack **Stewart** was a corporal (WX1839) in the Australian Infantry, attached to the 'Z' Special Unit. He was 35 years of age. His widow Juanita lived at Mosman Park, Western Australia.

Alfred **Warren** was a warrant officer 2nd class (VX52239) in the Australian Infantry, attached to the 'Z' Special Unit. He was 32 years of age. His widow Dorothy lived at Hawthorn, Victoria, Australia.

Others who were killed during Operation Rimau and are also buried at Kranji War Cemetery include Donald Montague Noel **Davidson** who was a lieutenant commander in the Royal Naval Volunteer Reserve, attached to the 'Z' Special Unit. He died on 18 October 1944 aged 35. His widow Nancy lived in Chelsea, London.

Archie Gordon Patrick **Campbell** was a corporal (QX5791) in the Australian Infantry, attached to the 'Z' Special Unit. There is some confusion around the date of Campbell's actual death. The Wikipedia website currently shows him dying in company with Davidson on 18 October 1944, either from his wounds or by swallowing his suicide pill. The Commonwealth War Graves Commission website records his death as having been 4 November 1944, which is a date which relates to a clash between members of the unit and a Japanese patrol which met at the island of Pulau Tapai. In the ensuing fight there were casualties on both sides. The only two casualties on the unit's side were Sub-Lieutenant Gregor **Riggs** and Sergeant Colin **Cameron**.

Harold Robert **Ross** was a lieutenant (325365) on the General List, attached to the 'Z' Special Unit. Having been part of the raiding team that had made good their escape from Singapore harbour after having set limpet charges on Japanese shipping, they were caught on Soreh Island. While trying to fight a rearguard action to allow four other members of their team to make good their escape, Ross, along with Lyon, was killed by a Japanese hand grenade. Stewart, who was with them, was captured and therefore would be one of the ten who were later executed. Ross was 24 years of age. His father, Thomas Spinks, was a retired lieutenant colonel with the Indian Medical Service.

Ivan **Lyon** DSO MBE was a lieutenant colonel (66175) in the Gordon Highlanders, attached to the 'Z' Special Unit. He was killed, aged 29, on 16 October in the same incident involving Ross. His father was Brigadier General Francis Lyon CB CMG CVO DSO. His widow Gabrielle lived in Farnham, Surrey.

Colin **Cameron** was a sergeant (VX81605) in the Australian Infantry, attached to 'Z' Special Unit, which was some achievement considering he was only 21 years of age. He was killed in action on 5 November 1944 during fighting with the Japanese on the island of Merapas. His parents lived at Wedderburn, Victoria, Australia.

James Gregor Mackintosh **Riggs**, a Scot by birth, was a sub-lieutenant in the Royal Naval Volunteer Reserve, attached to the 'Z' Special Unit. Like Cameron, who he would die next to fighting against the Japanese on the island of Merapas, he was also just 21 years of age when he was killed.

Archie Gordon Patrick **Campbell**, a corporal (QX5791) in the Australian Infantry, attached to the 'Z' Special Unit, died from his wounds in the same fighting on 4 November 1944 aged 24. His parents lived in Dalby, Queensland. Archie senior held both the DSO and the MC.

Able Seaman Frederick **Marsh**, who was one of the veterans of Operation Jaywick, was captured by the Japanese and would undoubtedly have faced the same fate as his ten colleagues who were beheaded, but he died of beriberi while being detained by the Japanese and awaiting trial. He is not shown as having been buried at the Kranji War Cemetery.

Jeffery **Willersdorf**, who was a warrant officer 2nd class (VX/81821) in the Australian Infantry, attached to the 'Z' Special Unit, died on 15 December 1944. He has no known grave but his name is commemorated on the Singapore Memorial which is within the Kranji War Cemetery. His parents lived in Essendon, Victoria, Australia.

Douglas Richard **Warne** was a private (QX/21698) in the Australian Infantry, attached to the 'Z' Special Unit, when he died on 15 December 1944. He was 24 years of age. He has no known grave and his name is commemorated on the Singapore Memorial at Kranji War Cemetery.

Colin Montague **Craft** was a corporal in the Australian Infantry, attached to the 'Z' Special Unit, when he died on 21 December 1944. He was 25 years of age. He has no known grave and his name is commemorated on the Singapore Memorial. His parents lived at Subiaco, Western Australia.

Hugo Joseph **Pace** was a 31-year-old lance corporal (QX20208) in the Australian Infantry, attached to the 'Z' Special Unit. He died on 15 December 1944. He has no known grave and his name is commemorated on the Singapore Memorial. At the time of his death, his parents were living in Port Said in Egypt.

Bruno Philip **Reymond**, a lieutenant in the Royal Australian Naval Reserve, was 31 years of age at the time of his death, which the Commonwealth War Graves Commission shows as being 21 December 1944, and his name is commemorated on the Plymouth Naval Memorial. While making good his escape from pursuing Japanese forces during Operation Rimau, he was killed on Pelapis Island, Indonesia. His widow Florence lived in Balmain, New South Wales, Australia.

Andrew William George **Huston** DSM was an able seaman (B/3312) in the Royal Australian Naval Reserve, attached to the 'Z' Special Unit. He was only 20 years of age when he died on 16 December 1944 and already a recipient of the Distinguished Service Medal, a remarkable achievement for one so young. His name is commemorated on the Plymouth Naval Memorial. His parents lived at Annerley, Queensland.

All twenty-three of the men who took part in Operation Rimau were either killed in action, were captured and executed, or escaped and subsequently died of their wounds; that much is known. Reymond, Willersdorf, Huston, Craft, Pace and Warne all died sometime between 15 and 21 December 1944, how and where exactly is not absolutely clear. Willersdorf, Craft, Pace and Warne are all commemorated on the Singapore Memorial, the final resting place of each man being unclear. Reymond and Huston, although both Australian servicemen and having died in the same timeframe, and one can only assume in the same locations as the others, are commemorated on the Plymouth Naval Memorial, thousands of miles away.

On 15 October 1944 Major Walter Chapman and Corporal Ronald Croton were on board HMS *Tantalus*, a T Class British Submarine on route for a rendezvous with anyone who had managed to survive and escape after Operation Rimau. Their destination was the island of Merapas where the supplies for the operation had been stored. The officer in charge of HMS *Tantalus* was Lieutenant Commander Hugh Mackenzie DSO. He had explicit orders: 'The Commanding Officer HMS *Tantalus* is responsible for the safety of the submarine which is to be his first consideration and has the discretion to cancel or postpone the operation at any time.' Mackenzie's main purpose was to conduct an offensive patrol in the South China Sea, primarily against the Japanese.

Chapman and Croton were dropped off by *Tantalus* in the early hours of 22 November 1944. Under the cover of darkness they carefully made their way to the agreed location to make contact with anyone who might have survived.

At first light, and having checked that there were no Japanese patrols waiting in the immediate vicinity for them, they began their search. All of the evidence suggested that members of the Operation Rimau team had been on the island in recent times. That evening, Chapman and Croton returned to HMS *Tantalus* and after a conversation with MacKenzie it was agreed that there was no purpose to be served in further waiting at Merapas any longer and if there had been any survivors from Operation Rimau, they had long moved on.

We know that six members of the team were still alive on 22 November 1944, but where they were and in what condition they were is unclear. Whether they were wounded or sick is not known.

Each and every one of them were very brave individuals who would have known the dangers that they were letting themselves in for long before they set off on their mission, unsung heroes if they survived, or staring death in the face if they failed.

# CHAPTER TWENTY ONE

# JAPANESE SURRENDER IN SINGAPORE

British forces landed back in Singapore at 11.30 am on 4 September 1945 in the shape of HMS *Sussex*. Following close behind into the safety of the harbour were a flotilla of other ships, including hospital ships for the large number of wounded, sick and disease-ridden prisoners of war and civilian internees they were expecting to find. There were also large cargo vessels carrying much needed food and other supplies which was ready to hand out to eager and grateful recipients. There were landing crafts, disembarking Indian troops and Royal Marines who were ready to go ashore and take over from the Japanese, who up until only a few days before had ruled the island by terror.

The Japanese had officially surrendered as a nation on 15 August 1945 when Emperor Hirohito gave a recorded radio address to his people. The signing of the official surrender document and its conditions took place on 2 September 1945 in Tokyo Bay on board the American Iowa class battleship USS *Missouri* with General of the Army, Douglas MacArthur, Supreme Allied Commander, signing on behalf of the Allies, and Foreign Minister Mamoru Shigemitsu signing on behalf of the Japanese.

The official surrender of Singapore and the subsequent document recording this act didn't take place until 12 September 1945 at the island's Municipal City Hall building. It is estimated that the crowds outside the building, which is situated immediately opposite the Padang, were in the region of 100,000 and included a combination of both Allied and Commonwealth troops along with masses of the island's local population.

The actual surrender had taken place eight days earlier on 4 September 1945 on board HMS *Sussex* in Keppel Harbour in Singapore, when General Seishiro Itagaki, Vice Admiral Fukudome, and their aides, had been invited on board the vessel by Lieutenant General Sir Philip Christison and Major General Robert Mansergh to discuss the surrender.

The matter hadn't always been as comfortable and as straightforward as that. Three days after the Japanese Emperor Hirohito had announced his country's surrender to the Allies, Itagaki flew out of Singapore on route to Saigon to speak with his direct boss Field Marshal Count Terauchi, who was in poor health and recovering from the effects of a stroke some months earlier. He was still officially the commander of the Japanese Southern Army and all forces in South East Asia.

It was abundantly clear that Itagaki did not want to surrender, and when he had initially received the order to do so he had ordered the men of the 25th Army on Singapore, who were under his control, to resist the Allies when they arrived back in Singapore. There were also, apparently, plans in place systematically to massacre all prisoners of war that were being held in Japanese captivity.

Thankfully, Terauchi appears to have managed to convince Itagaki that obeying the Emperor's direct order was the only thing that they could do in the circumstances. One would imagine that he would have made his argument even stronger by emphasising the point that if they failed to do as the Emperor had instructed them, they would be committing treason, which would not have been a very honourable thing for either of them to be doing.

After having finished his deliberations with Terauchi, Itagaki informed Mountbatten on 20 August that he and his troops on Singapore would abide by his Emperor's decision and that he was ready and waiting to receive further instructions for the Japanese surrender of Singapore.

The surrender document was signed on behalf of the Allied nations by Admiral Lord Louis Mountbatten, and General Seishiro Itagaki for the Japanese, deputising for Field Marshal Count Terauchi.

The surrender document still exists and the following is a replication of its content:

**Supreme Allied Command South East Asia.**

**Instrument of surrender of Japanese forces under the command or control of the Supreme Commander, Japanese Expeditionary Forces, Southern Regions, within the operational theatre of the Supreme Allied Commander, South East Asia.**

1.   *In pursuance of and in compliance with:*
     *(a) the Instrument of Surrender signed by the Japanese plenipotentiaries by command and on behalf of the Emperor of Japan, the Japanese Government and the Japanese Imperial General Headquarters at Tokyo on 2 September 1945;*

*(b) General Order No.1, promulgated at the same place on the same date;*

*(c) the local agreement made the Supreme Commander, Japanese Expeditionary Forces, Southern Regions, with the Supreme Allied Commander, South East Asia at Rangoon on 27 August 1945;to all of which Instrument of Surrender, General Order and Local Agreement this present Instrument is complementary and which it in no way supersedes, the Supreme Commander, Japanese Expeditionary Forces, Southern Regions (Field Marshall Count Terauchi) does hereby surrender unconditionally to the Supreme Allied Commander, South East Asia (Admiral The Lord Louis Mountbatten) himself and all Japanese sea, ground, air and auxiliary forces under his command or control and within the operational theatre of the Supreme Allied Commander, South East Asia.*

2. *The Supreme Allied Commander, Japanese Expeditionary Forces, Southern Regions, undertakes to ensure all orders and instructions that may be issued from time to time by the Supreme Allied Commander, South East Asia, or by any of his subordinate Naval, Military, or Air-Force Commanders of whatever rank acting in his name, are scrupulously and promptly obeyed by all Japanese sea, ground, air and auxiliary forces under the command or control of the Supreme Commander, Expeditionary Forces, Southern Regions, and within the operational theatre of the Supreme Allied Commander, South East Asia.*

3. *Any disobedience of, or delay or failure to comply with, orders or instructions issued by the Supreme Allied Commander, South East Asia, or issued on his behalf by any of his subordinate Naval, Military, or Air Force Commanders of whatever rank, and any action which the Supreme Military Allied Commander, South East Asia, or his subordinate Commanders' action on his behalf, may determine to be detrimental to the Allied Powers, will be dealt with as the Supreme Allied Commander, South East Asia may decide.*

4. *This instrument takes effect from the time and date of signing.*

5. *This instrument is drawn up in the English Language, which is the only authentic version. In any case of doubt to intention or meaning, the decision of the Supreme Allied Commander,*

*South East Asia is final. It is the responsibility of the Supreme Commander Japanese Expeditionary Forces, Southern Regions, to make such translations into Japanese as he may require.*

*Signed at Singapore at 0341 hours (GMT) on 12 September 1945.*
*Seishiro Itagaki*
*(for) Supreme Commander*
*Japanese Expeditionary Forces*
*Southern Regions.*

*Louis Mountbatten*
*Supreme Allied Commander*
*South East Asia.*

# CHAPTER TWENTY TWO

# SINGAPORE WAR CRIMES TRIALS AND THE AFTERMATH

The war crimes trials, with the defendants being mainly Japanese military personnel, took place throughout South East Asia, in Tokyo, Yokohama, Manila, Penang and Singapore. They opened in Singapore on 21 January 1946 and came to an end in December 1948. Not all of the defendants were tried for crimes that had taken place in Singapore; quite a few had been committed at other locations. They had been carried out by Japanese officers and soldiers in the Andaman Islands, Java, Horoekoe Island, Babelthuap Palau, Palembang, Burma, Sarawak, Siam, Borneo, the Philippines and Port Blair.

Case No. 235/843 relates to five members of the Imperial Japanese Army who were stationed at the Oxley Rise Kempeitai station. In January 1944 they arrested three local men who they believed had assisted in the escape of an unnamed prisoner of war. The three men, Lee Keok Leong, Lee Tee Tee and Lee Eng Tong were then interrogated and tortured for three weeks at the Oxley Rise station before being taken to Outram Road Prison. Lee Tee Tee and Lee Eng Tong both died while in Japanese custody, the former in July 1944 and the latter in January 1945. Four out of five of the Kempeitai were found guilty on the evidence of the survivor, Lee Keok Leong, even though only one of the Japanese soldiers, Sergeant Matsumoto Mitsugi, admitted taking part in any of the beatings. Mitsugi, Lieutenant Yamaguchi Akuni, Sergeant Uekihara Susumi and Sergeant Shimomura Tomohei, were sentenced to death and hung. Sergeant Major Ikeda Saiichi was found not guilty of charges and acquitted.

Another trial that took place in Singapore in relation to war crimes which had taken place there was Case No. 235/975. It was referred to as the Otsuka case, but there were in fact forty-three defendants. Those concerned had been charged with committing war crimes at the Outram Road Prison between 16 February 1942 and 15 August 1945 relating to their ill treatment and neglect of British, American and Dutch prisoners of war as well as local civilian internees who were incarcerated at Outram Road Prison. This had resulted in the deaths of thirteen British prisoners of war, four Dutch prisoners of war, and twenty-two civilian internees. The trial took thirty-one days in total to complete, beginning on 8 July 1946 and finishing 10 October 1946. Four of the accused were found not guilty and acquitted. Five received life sentences. One received a seventeen year sentence, five received twelve year sentences, six received ten year sentences, with the remainder receiving sentences of between one and eight years.

After having experienced three years of Japanese occupation between 1942 and 1945, a time which saw numerous acts of brutality meted out, especially to Chinese men in Singapore, there are not too many who can miss the obvious poignancy of Japanese soldiers having to face trials for war crimes they committed in the same country.

The main Japanese politicians, including the Prime Minister, Hideki Tojo, who was also the commander of the Kwantung Army, Koki Hirota, who was the Foreign Minister, Seishiro Itagaki, the War Minister, and Heitaro Kimura, were all tried in Tokyo for crimes against peace. All were found guilty and executed. They were hung at Sugamo prison in Ikebukuro. Their collective crime was the brutal mistreatment of American and Filipino prisoners of war in their care.

Some 5,700 Japanese military personnel were tried after the war for general 'war crimes' and 'crimes against humanity', which fortunately for the defendants who were found guilty, did not include the death penalty. In total some 919 Japanese were tried by the Allied powers; 222 were found guilty and executed for their war time crimes; another 53 received life sentences; 477 were given lengthy prison sentences, and 105 of the defendants were tried and found not guilty of the charges that had been brought against them.

One case on the first day of the trials saw nine officers and men of the Imperial Japanese Army tried and found guilty of the murder of a group of Indian prisoners of war. Eight of them received lengthy prison sentences while the other received the death penalty for his crimes. The nine men were Captain Gozawa Saidachi, Captain Okusawa Ken, Lieutenant Kamiyuki Nakamura, Sergeant Major Tanno Shozo, Sergeant Major Ono Tadasu, Sergeant Yubi Junichiro, Corporal Osuki Makoto, Corporal Ashiya Tomotsu and Lance Corporal Chiba Masami.

Lieutenant Colonel Sleeman of the 15th/16th Lancers and Major Fairburn of the Rifle Brigade had the unenviable job of defending the accused, while Lieutenant Colonel Lazarus and Captain Hibbert, both of the Royal Army Service Corps, made up the prosecuting team. The three-man bench who would ultimately decide whether the accused would live or die for their crimes comprised Lieutenant Colonel Colman of the Royal Army Ordnance Corps, who was also the Court's President, Major Gay of the Cameronians, and Captain Koli of the Indian Army.

The war crimes trials which took place in Singapore included both Japanese military personnel as well as civilians of different nationalities. They were watched closely by the world's press and in Britain there was understandably a lot of interest in the proceedings.

The *Western Morning Post* dated Saturday 5 January 1946 carried the following report:

### Singapore's Fall
### General Bennett – No Action
### Commission Report

*No action is contemplated against Lieutenant-General Bennett, former Australian commander in Malaya, it was stated here tonight, after the Government Commission reported that he was not justified in relinquishing his command and leaving Singapore at the time of its fall in February 1942.*

*Although the enquiry findings justified a Court-Martial charge, high Army circles said it was felt no good purpose would be served by such a move.*

*The Commission's report added that General Bennett 'acted from a sense of high patriotism, according to his conception of his duty to Australia.'*

*Mr Justice Ligertwood found that at the time General Bennett left Singapore he was not a prisoner of war in the sense of being a soldier under duty to escape.*

*Mr Justice Ligertwood was unable to agree that General Bennett's command was ended by the unconditional surrender. There were still things to be doing under the capitulation.*

*General Bennett commented, 'General Percival surrendered unconditionally and admits it. The Japanese admit it also. How there can be capitulation, which is surrender with conditions when both sides say there was unconditional surrender, is beyond me.'*

Maybe in an attempt to lighten the severity of his earlier comments about General Bennett, Mr Justice Ligertwood later added the following:

*General Bennett was the first Australian to meet the Japanese in battle, thereby acquiring valuable information and experience. General Bennett genuinely believed that Australia was in peril and that it was of vital importance that he should return to take part in its defence.*

The fact that in November 1945 the Australian Prime Minister decided to appoint a Royal Commission into Bennett's actions in leaving Singapore when he did speaks volumes for what the general feeling must have been amongst the Australian public about his actions. In essence the enquiry found him guilty, his actions deemed suitable for a court martial, which was not proceeded with.

One wonders how the 2,000 men of the Australian 8th Division who were under his command at the time collectively felt about his untimely escape, which took place on the evening of 15 February 1942. He handed over the command of the 8th Division to Brigadier Cecil Callaghan and made good his escape, eventually arriving back in Melbourne, Australia on 2 March 1942.

The issue about Bennett's actions at Singapore only came to light after the war when Percival and Callaghan were released from captivity. Percival wrote a letter accusing Bennett of relinquishing his command of the Australian 8th Division without his permission. Percival gave the letter to Callaghan who took it back to Australia with him where he passed it on to General Thomas Blamey.

The *Yorkshire Evening Post* of Friday 11 January 1946 covered the story of the death of Sapper Ernest Glover:

### Hemsworth War Prisoner Died
### Jap Camp Chief to be charged

*Sapper Ernest Glover of Hemsworth is one of two British war prisoners who died in a camp in Japan.*

*The other prisoner was Pte. Raymond Suttle of Hadleigh. They were in a prison camp at Hakodate on Hokkaido, Japan's northernmost island.*

*Maichi Hirate, commandant of the camp, will be charged before a United States Military Commission on Monday with causing the deaths of Glover and Suttle through maltreatment.*

*Hirate, the fourth alleged war criminal to be tried in Japan, faces a long list of other crimes.*

*Sapper Glover, who was 44, was the youngest son of Mrs Wren and the late Mr J T Glover, of Barnsley Road, Hemsworth, and he enlisted eight years ago. He was captured at the fall of Singapore. His mother has received notification from the War Office that he died on January 3, 1944, as a result of primary acute osteomyelitis of the left tibia and secondary pyaemia. He was a miner at South Kirkby Colliery, and after a serious accident at work decided to join the Army.*

Osteomyelitis is the infection and inflammation of the bone or bone marrow and pyaemia is a type of septicaemia that results from widespread abscesses which, before the introduction of antibiotics, was nearly always fatal.

The *Hartlepool Mail* of Wednesday 16 January 1946 carried the following piece about the kind offer from an airman who was still serving in Singapore at the time:

### The Fallen heroes of Singapore

*Hartlepool's people who have relatives buried in the British war cemetery at Singapore will be interested in a kind offer made through Mr R E Read, of 47 Belmont Gardens, West Hartlepool, by an RAF man who is stationed at the Far East base. The airman offers to take photographs of the graves of any local men buried there and send them to the relatives, and Mr Read is prepared to forward names, addresses and regimental numbers to his friend for that purpose. In his letter the airman relates how recently the men in his unit subscribed for two wreaths which, at an impressive ceremony, were placed on the graves of the British and Australian dead, and it was then that the thought of sending photographs to relatives occurred to him.*

That was such a considerate thing for this airman to do because for most relatives the cost of travel to Singapore to visit the grave of their loved one would have been beyond their financial capabilities.

The *Aberdeen Journal* dated Wednesday 16 January 1946 contained the following article about the Singapore war crimes trials that started five days later:

### RASC Driver rose to Lieutenant-Colonel

*Lieut. Colonel Alan Smith, a young Aberdeen solicitor, will preside over one of several military courts, to open in Singapore within the next week or two, to try Japanese war criminals.*

*His promotion to that post marks the climax of a remarkable Army career.*

*In 1941 Colonel Alan Smith left his civilian work as a partner in the firm of Mollinson and Smith solicitors and joined the RASC.*

*For a year or two he was a driver then a Corporal. About a year ago he was an officer cadet. Then he signed himself 'Lieutenant' in a letter which he wrote to an Aberdeen friend not very long ago. The next letter to the same friend announced his promotion to the rank of Lieut. Colonel.*

> *About 2000 Jap war criminals, including several Generals, await trial by the courts to be opened in Singapore, and many hundreds have yet to be rounded up.*
>
> *The court over which Colonel Smith will preside will sit in the building of the Supreme Court of Justice in Malaya. Colonel Smith, who is thirty-five, is a law graduate of Aberdeen University. His mother lives at 23 Oakhill Road, Aberdeen.*
>
> *For several years he was the deputy procurator-fiscal at Fort William. He has accepted the Singapore court post on condition that it will not delay his return to civilian life. He is in Group 31.*

The *Western Morning News* of Thursday, 17 January 1946, covered the story from Singapore about Chinese people living on the island wanting General Tomoyuki Yamashita extradited to Singapore to stand trial for war crimes that he had committed during the Sook Ching massacre.

### Massacred Chinese

*The Chinese in Singapore are demanding the extradition of Gen. 'Tiger' Yamashita for trial as a war criminal. A formal request will be placed before the Far Eastern Advisory Council. The Chinese say that during the early stages of the Japanese occupation 50,000 Singapore Chinese were massacred.*

General Tomoyuki Yamashita was the officer who had been in charge of the Japanese 25th Army when they had invaded Malaya on 8 December 1941. He took the surrender of Percival at Singapore on 15 February 1942 and was in charge of Japanese forces in Singapore when atrocities such as the murders at Alexandra Hospital and the Sook Ching massacre took place.

Having surrendered to the Americans on 2 September 1945 in the Philippines, Yamashita was subsequently put on trial in Manila for war crimes committed both in the Philippines and Singapore. His trial started on 29 October 1945 and ended on 7 December 1945 with him being found guilty as charged. Despite appeals made by his legal team that went all the way up to the Supreme Court of the United States of America, and even an appeal of clemency to the President of the United States, Yamashita was executed by hanging on 23 February 1946 at Los Baños, Laguna prison camp which is about thirty miles south of Manila.

There remains to this day some controversy concerning his execution.

The *Derby Daily* Telegraph of Friday 18 January 1946 reported the proposed arrest of 110 Japanese war crimes suspects:

### Arrest of 110 Japs ordered

*General MacArthur, Supreme Allied Commander in Japan, has ordered the arrest of 110 more Japanese war crimes suspects.*

*Among them is General Takeji Vachi, former Chief of Staff in the Philippines. Most of the others are camp guards.*

*Major-General Eugen Ott, Nazi Ambassador to Tokyo at the time of the Pearl Harbor attack, has been arrested, Chinese authorities in Peking announced today.*

*British Counsel will defend Japanese who will face charges of war crimes in trials starting at Singapore on Monday.*

The *Dundee Evening Telegraph*, Monday, 21 January 1946, contained yet another report of alleged Japanese brutality towards prisoners of war who had been held in their control:

### 117 Died after Jap horror voyage

*More than 500 Indians, after a 34 day sea voyage from Singapore to Palau, 600 miles from New Guinea, in a ship which they scarcely had room to sit, were starved and beaten until 117 died, it was alleged when trials of Japanese war criminals opened here today,*

*The ten closely shorn Japanese officers and NCOs, guarded in the dock by a British Sergeant with a loaded Sten gun, pleaded not guilty to ill-treating them.*

*The prosecution alleged that on the voyage food was infested with maggots and drinking water was very difficult to get, even in small quantities. Some victims of the daily beatings at Palau sustained permanent injury, and by January, 1945, the Indian prisoners were at starvation level.*

*Indians were forced to dig a trench beside which a Japanese officer, Lieut. Nakamura, beheaded one of their number.*

The *Dundee Evening Telegraph* dated Tuesday, 22 January, 1946 covered the following story:

### Japs punished POW, 'Out of kindness'

*The War Crimes Court at Singapore today granted the prosecutor's application to treat a Japanese Sergeant Major, Tomeyama*

> *Mitsugi, as a hostile witness when he said the Japanese punished Indian prisoners of war out of kindness to save them from a 'different handling.'*
>
> *Mitsugi was giving evidence in the trial of ten Japanese officers and NCOs charged with ill-treating Indian Prisoners.*
>
> *He added that as he was not a member of the Japanese Police he could not tell what the 'different handling' might be. The prosecutor suggested that the cryptic smile on Tomeyama's lips showed that he understood the methods he was talking about.*

The meaning of the phrase 'different handling' is not clear, but as it is mentioned specifically in relation to Indian soldiers, it can only be assumed that there is a racial connotation to it. The inference by the trial judge was that Tomeyama Mitsugi certainly understood its relevance.

The *Dundee Courier* of Thursday, 24 January 1946, contained the following report:

### Presumed killed at Singapore

> *Mr G Ritchie, 53 Hill Street, Dundee, has received intimation that his eldest son, Pte Glenalvon Ritchie, RAMC, who was reported missing in February 1942, is now presumed to have lost his life while fighting in Singapore at that time.*
>
> *Employed in the plumbers' shop in Caledon Shipyard before joining up in 1937, he went to China in 1938, and three years later was transferred to Malaya. Born in Dundee, he attended Dens Road and Rockwell schools. He was 23.*

The Commonwealth War Graves Commission website shows Private (7263686) Glenalvon Edwin Ritchie as having being killed in action during fighting in Singapore on either 14 or 15 February 1942, that he was 23 years of age and a member of the Royal Army Medical Corp. He has no known grave and his name is commemorated on the Singapore Memorial which is located at the Kranji War Cemetery.

The memorial has the names of more than 24,000 Commonwealth servicemen who have no known grave, and in many cases no known date, location or circumstances of how they died. The official date of death that has been accorded to them relates to the date from which they were known to have been missing or the date on which they were known to have been captured.

The *Yorkshire Evening Post* newspaper from Friday, 25 January 1946, reported on casualties from the Yorkshire area who had been fighting with British forces in Burma, Malaya and Singapore.

### Yorkshire casualties

*Captain Mark Leigh, son of Mr and Mrs H Leigh, Grange Avenue, Leeds, died in British General Hospital, Singapore, on December 26. He was Army welfare officer attached to the YMCA in Singapore. He was a talented cellist, and an old pupil of Arthur Haynes, first cellist with the Northern Philharmonic Orchestra.*

*Mrs Dorothy White, Stanley Hall Gardens, Aberford Road, Wakefield, has news that her husband, Gunner Walter White, serving with the 85th Anti-Tank Regiment, RA, in Malaya, when Singapore fell, died from pneumonia while a prisoner of war on June 29, 1942, in Roberts hospital, Changi, Singapore. In civil life he was head gardener of the Wakefield Mental and Pinderfields hospital.*

*Pte. G N R Fish, Goole Road, Snaith, reported missing in May 1942, is now assumed to have lost his life in Burma.*

The *Dundee Evening Telegraph* of Tuesday, 29 January 1946, reported about the general strike which took place both in Singapore and the state of Johore, just across the causeway in Malaya:

### General strike in Singapore

*A general strike began today in Singapore and Johore, called by the labour unions in protest against the arrest of certain union officials and the imprisonment of Soong Kwong, a former secretary-general of the Selangor Anti-Japanese Union.*

*Thousands of shopkeepers, transport workers, municipal labourers, hospital and domestic staff, and hotel servants are involved.*

*There have been several strikes in Singapore during the past four months, but this is the first time that the domestic staffs of private houses, military and civilian messes, cafes and hotels have stopped work.*

The strike lasted for only two days before Singapore's labour unions called it off.

The *Hartlepool Mail* of Wednesday, 30 January 1946, highlighted the fact that besides the war crimes trials which were taking place in

Singapore, there were still recriminations about what had happened on the island which led to the British surrender and the subsequent occupation by the Japanese:

### The Singapore Surrender
### Sydney Paper urges
### 'No witch hunt'

*The* Sydney Sun *said today that the Singapore surrender should not become a 'witch' hunt for victims and reputations.*

*'It is timely that a full enquiry should be held into the whole sad story of neglect, complacency, and general unpreparedness, and that Lieut-General Gordon Bennett, former GOC Australian Forces in Malaya, should represent the division he commanded,' added the paper.*

The *Lancashire Evening Post* dated Tuesday, 5 February 1946, reported the following sad story:

### Died in Singapore

*Mr & Mrs Greenhaigh of 61 Nevett Street, New Hall Lane, Preston, Lancashire, have been notified of the death in hospital at Singapore, while a prisoner of war of their son, Lance Corporal Ernest Greenhaigh of the Manchester Regiment. He is reported to have died from dysentery on September 20, 1942. He attended St Matthews School and before joining up in 1940 was employed at Messers Berry's, Kirkham Street. His younger brother has served in the Navy for over five years.*

The *Essex Newsman* of Tuesday, 5 February 1946, carried the following story of brotherly love:

### Brothers meet in Singapore

*Two brothers, LAC Samuel Francis (Frank) Meadows, RAF, and Pte William Meadows 1st Northampton Reg., have met in Singapore after four years of service without seeing one another. Frank went first, to India. William of the 14th Army, followed. Both were sent to Burma, then on to Malaya, and on to Singapore. One day Frank who was in hospital, was sitting on his bed, when in walked his brother William, and a happy re-union took place.*

*Frank, aged 23, has been in the Services five years, four of which have been spent overseas; and William aged 22, not quite so long, mostly abroad. They have nine brothers and sisters. Their parents*

*Mr and Mrs S Meadows, live at Mill Green, Ingatestone. Frank is married and his wife, who expects him home in the summer, resides at 17 Springfield Park Road, Chelmsford.*

This I found particularly poignant as I have a photograph of my two sons taken at Camp Bastion in Afghanistan in September 2012. My elder son had just arrived at the start of his six-month tour of the region, while the younger one was preparing to return home after having completed his second six-month tour. As they were not in the same unit, there was some polite banter and rivalry between the two of them.

The *Aberdeen Journal* dated Thursday, 7 February 1946, carried the following report.

### Fine work in Singapore

*A fine job is being done by the 2nd Reconnaissance Regiment in restoring the British atmosphere to Selarang Barracks, Singapore, where the Japs held sway for a few years.*

*Helping in the good work are two Aberdeen men, L/Cpl. D Watt, 68 Holburn Street and Trooper W Carr, 39 Mount Street.*

*The 2nd Reconnaissance Regiment, formerly the 6th Battalion, The Loyal Regiment, recently moved from Malaya to take part in garrisoning Singapore Island.*

*The Regiment became the 2nd Division's reconnaissance unit in 1941, and with it was bound for Madagascar when it was diverted to internal security work in India.*

*The Regiment distinguished itself at the crossing of Irrawaddy, thirty miles west of Mandalay. Once the bridgehead was established, it broke through and was first to link up with the 20th Division.*

The *Dundee Evening Telegraph* of Thursday, 7 February 1946, carried the following report:

### British Court's death sentence on woman.

*A British officer's court, today passed sentence of death on two civilians, Doreen Wales De Silva and her husband, Manuel De Silva, for having allegedly worked with the Japanese Secret Police.*

*The Court made a recommendation for mercy. The sentence will be subject to confirmation by the General Officer Commanding Malaya.*

*The De Silvas who come from the Portuguese colony of Goa, India, were alleged to have given information against six dance hostesses*

*and a man employed at the German club in Singapore, who were*
*then tortured by the Japanese Gestapo.*

*Elizabeth Gomes, one of the hostesses, told the court that she*
*falsely confessed to being a British spy after being beaten with a stick,*
*tortured with electric wires fastened to her fingers and having her*
*ears burnt with cigarettes.*

*Today's were the first war crimes sentences passed against civilians.*

It was sad to note that even after the war had finished and with the
events of the Japanese occupation still fresh in the memories of those
residents of Singapore who had lived through those dark days, peace
and tranquillity had still not totally returned to become a part of everyday life on the island.

On Friday, 15 February 1946, the fourth anniversary of the fall of
Singapore to Japanese forces, the *Nottingham Evening Post* reported the
following:

### Singapore clash
### Charges against the Police

*One man was shot and several injured when police and Chinese were*
*involved in a clash near the Bras Basah Road today, the date for the*
*proposed demonstrations by local unions to commemorate the fall of*
*Singapore to the Japanese four years ago.*

*Later, an official statement said that 'serious charges' had been*
*made against the conduct of certain members of the police, and that*
*an immediate and searching enquiry had been ordered by SEAC*
*Headquarters.*

*Last night the police raided the offices of the three organisations*
*planning today's demonstration, and detained a number of people for*
*questioning. Several were later released.*

Three days later, on 18 February 1946, an article appeared in the
*Aberdeen Journal* announcing that the Singapore police had been exon-
erated from acting with any brutality. The announcement was made by
Admiral Lord Louis Mountbatten, the Supreme Allied Commander,
who fully endorsed the findings of the official enquiry.

The S*underland Daily Echo and Shipping Gazette* of Saturday, 23
February 1946, reported the following:

### The Tiger of Malaya hanged.

*General Yamashita, the Tiger of Malaya and conqueror of Singapore,*
*was today hanged as a war criminal.*

> *Yamashita, who was sentenced to death by a US Military Tribunal*
> *for permitting atrocities when he was Japanese Commander-in-Chief*
> *in the Philippines, met his death on a scaffold erected at a place 35*
> *miles outside Manila.*
>
> *Two other Japanese war criminals were executed at the same time.*
>
> *The General's last words were: 'I will pray for the Emperor's long*
> *life and his prosperity for ever.'*
>
> *As he stepped up to the scaffold accompanied by a priest and an*
> *interpreter, he appeared calm and stoic according to the US Army*
> *announcement of the execution.*
>
> *Yamashita was responsible for the deaths of 25,000 men women*
> *and children and for the mass executions of US prisoners.*
>
> *An hour after Yamashita was hanged, Lieut.-Col. Seiichi Ohta,*
> *head of the dreaded secret police in Manila and the most hated man*
> *in the Philippines, and Akuma Higashiji, a civilian interpreter, fol-*
> *lowed him to the gallows.*
>
> *Higashiji, who during his trial laughed as witnesses were describing*
> *his torture of civilians, was the only one of the three who showed signs*
> *of nervousness, crying 'Good-bye for ever' as he went to the gallows.*
>
> *The execution of the three Japanese was held in the utmost secrecy.*

The *Gloucestershire Echo* newspaper of 20 February 1946 carried a report about two members of the Kempeitai who were to be hung after being found guilty of war crimes:

### Two Jap Secret Police to die

> *Two members of the Japanese Kempeitai Secret Police were sen-*
> *tenced to death by a Singapore War Crimes Court today on charges*
> *of beating, torturing, and causing the death of Chinese civilians, says*
> *a Singapore message.*
>
> *The men were Warrant Officer Hirazawa Atsusi and Staff*
> *Sergeant Shin Shigetoshi.*
>
> *Two other members of the Kempeitai were sentenced to terms of 14*
> *and 5 years' imprisonment.*
>
> *Atsusi, appealing for mercy, told the court, 'I apologise for my*
> *crimes. I promise to be a good citizen in future.'*

Atsusi's appeal fell on death ears and along with Shigetoshi he was executed.

Five members of the Kempeitai were actually on trial. Staff Sergeant Terada Takao, who was acquitted, had been charged along with his four colleagues of

*Committing a War Crime in that they together in Singapore on or after 20 Oct 44 in violation of the laws and usages of war, being in the service of the occupying power, conspired and acted towards and were concerned together in the unlawful arrest and confinement and in the beating, torture and maltreatment of Lam Keong Kong, Wong Pin and Lam Nai Fook, civilian residents of Singapore, in consequence whereof the said Wong Pin died.*

Corporal Hase Ryosoku faced the same charge along with a similar charge whereby another civilian resident of Singapore, Lam Nai Peng, died. He only received a sentence of five years.

Private Murata Yoshitaro was found guilty of the above two charges, which resulted in the deaths of two civilians, as well as a third charge where he was found guilty of beating, torturing and maltreating a civilian resident of Singapore. His sentence was fourteen years' imprisonment.

The *Gloucestershire Echo*, thankfully, reported a lot of what was happening at the war crimes trials in Singapore. Their edition of Monday, 15 April 1946, had the following report on its front page:

*Sentence of death was passed today, at the end of the biggest wars crimes trial Singapore has yet staged, on a Japanese Lieutenant-Colonel, a Warrant Officer and five Sergeant-Majors and Sergeants.*

*In addition, a Chinese interpreter was condemned to death.*

*Three other Japanese were sentenced to life imprisonment, one to 15 years and another eight, and a Chinese interpreter to eight years.*

*Six Japanese were acquitted on the grounds of mistaken identity or benefit of the doubt.*

The *Gloucestershire Echo* newspaper reported on Thursday, 25 April 1946, that two unnamed Japanese sailors had been sentenced to death after having being found guilty at the war crimes trials in Singapore of beating and torturing two civilians at Port Blair in the Andaman Islands in June 1945. The specific details of what injuries the two sailors had inflicted upon their victims before they had died were not included in the report.

The *Taunton Courier and Western Advertiser* dated Saturday, 20 July 1946, carried the following sad news:

### Killed in Singapore
### Taunton mother receives official news

*Mrs B Hooper, of 17 Charter Road, Taunton, has been officially informed that her third son, Gnr. Ronald Claude K Brown, RA, was killed in Singapore in February 1942. He had been previously reported missing since February 15th of that year.*

*Born in October 1917, at Taunton, Ronald joined the Army when he was 17. Before then he had been employed at Messrs. Shirley & Power Ltd, grocers at Taunton. At about the time he joined the Army he made a brave rescue of a dog from the River Tone.*

The *Morpeth Herald Newspaper* of Friday, 2 August 1946, included the following extremely interesting letter under the heading

### News from Singapore
### The wheels of Justice

*Dear Colonel Swinton,*

*I am sure you will want to know the destinies of some of our yellow friends.*

*Shortly after I got here, Komai and Ejima were hanged for the murder of Hawley and Armitage, and in the same connection Watauabe, Sekichi and Urakawa got jug for life and Major Cheda got eight years; Watauabe Masao, the decent sergeant from 1 group, got off with a nominal sentence. Takasahki and Kaneshiro (the 'Frog' and the 'Undertaker') are to be hanged shortly for the killing of Howard and Pomeroy and four British other ranks of your Regiment.*

*Mizutani is to be hanged for the murder of Fusilier Wanty. Adah and Nebusawa are to be hanged for atrocities at Chunkai and elsewhere, and for sending sick men back up country to work. Tarimoto has got imprisonment for life, and lucky to get away with that. Noguchi's trial is coming up soon, and also Kokubo (alias 'Drunken Bill'). I doubt if he will be hanged though from what I have seen of the evidence. A crowd of Group IV are coming up soon.*

*The 'Kanyo Kid' (alias Osuki), 'Dr Death' (Medical Serg Okada), Suzuki, the Group Commander and a number of Koreans, including 'Donald Duck,' 'The Mad Mongol,' 'The Boy Bastard' and 'The Silver Bullet.'*

*Nobusawa tried to cut his stomach open with a safety razor blade before the trial and on being sentenced to death, threw himself out of a window but survived with a broken leg.*

*Sugasawa's trial isn't coming up for a while yet.*

Colonel Swinton, to whom the letter had originally been sent, was with the 9th Battalion, Royal Northumberland Fusiliers, a Territorial Army Unit which had first arrived in Singapore on 5 February 1942 on board the French troopship the *Felix Roussel*.

Not all Japanese soldiers who faced a war crimes trial were found guilty. *The Gloucestershire Echo* reported the following case on its front cover on Tuesday, 1 October 1946:

### Jap Major acquitted on war crime charge.

*Major Katsumura, officer commanding the Kempeitai, or the Japanese Secret Police, at Buitenzorg, Java, during the Japanese occupation, was today acquitted by the Australian War Crimes Court here, on a charge which if it had been heard at Nuremburg might have ended with a guilty verdict, says a Singapore message.*

*He was accused of complicity in the unlawful killing of three Allied PoWs and a Dutch woman in September 1943, on orders from Kempeitai HQ in Batavia.*

*Lieutenant-Colonel C R E Jennings, presiding, said that the Court had been guided by the amendment to Australian military law which said that soldiers under conditions of war discipline could not be expected to weigh the legal merits of orders they received.*

*Five of Major Katsumura's subordinates were acquitted with him. When the acquittal finding was given, Major Katsumura and his men smiled, bowed, and clicked heels in Japanese military fashion.*

The *Dundee Evening Telegraph* reported the following on Tuesday, 15 October 1946:

*Lieutenant-General Kumakichi Harada, Commander in Chief Japanese forces in Java, is being tried before an Australian War Crimes court at Singapore.*

*With three other Japanese officers and a Japanese Sergeant-Major, Harada is charged with unlawfully killing three Australian airmen, survivors of a crashed Catalina air craft.*

*The prosecution said that three flight Sergeants, named Ryan, Brown and Vetter, after being brought to Batavia late in 1944, became a definite embarrassment to the Japanese as they were aware of the progress of the Pacific war.*

*Harada decided that it was inadvisable to keep them alive, and on February 5, 1945, they were beheaded beside their graves at Tandjong Priok.*

The *Gloucestershire Echo* newspaper of Tuesday, 27 January 1948, ran with the following headline:

## Jap General to Die.

*Singapore, Tuesday. The War Crimes Trial Court at Changi has passed sentence of death by hanging on Major-General Sasa Akira, for ordering the shooting of four British prisoners of war who had tried to escape from Takirin camp during the construction of the Burma-Siam railway in February 1943.*

Japanese military personnel of all ranks had a nationalistic attitude towards enemy combatants who surrendered in battle. They saw it as a dishonourable thing to do, having been brought up to believe that to die in battle was not only honourable for them but for their families as well. These strongly held beliefs had a direct effect on how they treated prisoners of war, no matter which country they were from.

In the main, Japanese soldiers mistreated Allied prisoners of war in their care with a barbaric sadism and showed absolutely no respect for the sanctity of human life. The number of beheadings of prisoners of war, or occasions when they were bayoneted to death for the most minor of infringements, happened too many times for them to have been isolated and ill-disciplined actions by out-of-control Japanese soldiers. I have not found one single case where a Japanese soldier, of any rank, was disciplined by his superior officer for having carried out what we would regard as an atrocity. The only conclusion it is possible to reach is that it was a matter of Japanese military policy to treat prisoners of war in this way.

The Geneva Convention of 1929 set guidelines on how prisoners of war were to be treated by their captors. Japan and Russia did not sign the treaty.

Just so as to balance things out, I thought that it was only right and proper to mention the following incident that took place during the early part of 1945:

In 1945, Lieutenant Masaichi Kikuchi, of the Imperial Japanese Army, commanded an airfield defence unit in Singapore when he was allocated 300 Indian prisoners of war as part of a labour force. When they had been handed over to him, the Japanese officer who was responsible for their delivery, said to Kikuchi, 'When you've finished, you can do what you like with them,' then casually added, 'If I was you I'd shove them into a tunnel with a few demolition charges.' When two of these prisoners subsequently escaped, only to be recaptured and returned to Kikuchi a short time later, he did not have them executed as he should have done. One can only assume he was a fair and honourable man who knew in his heart that this was not the right thing to do. His prisoners' actions were probably no different to what he would have done if he had been a prisoner of war and found himself with the opportunity to escape from his captors.

The following story from the *Gloucestershire Echo* dated Monday, 18 October 1948, was about the Bishop of Singapore, Dr John Leonard Wilson, and his internment by the Japanese authorities during their occupation of Singapore.

### Tortured Bishop to be Dean

*The Bishop of Singapore, Dr J L Wilson, who for eight months during the occupation was imprisoned, flogged, tortured and ill-treated by the Japanese, will become Dean of Manchester next year, his commissary the Reverend J W J Steele announced in St Andrews Cathedral, Singapore, last night.*

*Dr Wilson, formerly Arch-Deacon of Hong Kong, gave evidence at a Singapore War Crime Trial in April 1946, when sentence of death was passed on a Japanese Lieutenant-Colonel, and six non-commissioned officers.*

*It was stated that he was given 200 strokes in one flogging before he fainted, and was unable to walk for three months.*

*Dr Wilson, who is 51, is at present returning to Singapore by sea from a seven months' tour of Britain and Holland.*

Dr Wilson was the Bishop of Singapore for seven years between 1941 and 1948.

The unusually named newspaper, the *Yorkshire Post and Leeds Intelligencer* dated Saturday, 26 October 1946, contained the following report on its front cover:

### Beheaded Australians:
### Japanese Commander in Chief to die
(Singapore, Friday)

*Sentence of death was passed by a War Crimes court in Singapore today on Lieutenant General Kumakichi Harada, Japanese Commander in Chief, and on his intelligence staff officer, Lieutenant-Colonel Kazuo Masugi, for ordering the beheading of three Australian airmen, survivors of a crashed Catalina, who were brought to Batavia in 1944.*

The inhumanity of which certain individuals are capable can come to the surface in a time of war. Men can become dehumanised by what they see, are involved in or surrounded by. Some men who in normal everyday life are painters, bank managers, solicitors, milkmen and the like, can become monsters when sent off to war, suddenly capable of carrying out extreme acts of violence that they would otherwise find abhorrent as a civilian. There certainly were plenty of examples of this that came out during the Singapore war crimes trials; men who wouldn't warrant a second glance if passed in the street back home in Japan, but when placed in a uniform and sent off to war were changed forever.

# CHAPTER TWENTY THREE

# THE INTERNATIONAL RED CROSS – POST WAR

Once the war was over, the work of the ICRC was far from finished. Their representative in Singapore, Mr H Schweizer, along with colleagues from across South East Asia, now had the massive task of dealing with both sides at the same time. They initially had to gain access to all of the prisoner of war camps which held British, Australian and Indian troops and deal with the wellbeing of those who had been held captive. On top of this they also had to look after the numerous civilian internment camps as well. Once all of the Allied troops had left and been repatriated to their homelands, the ICRC had to go back in to many of the same camps and deal in the exact same way with the Japanese military personnel, who were now captives rather than captors.

On 26 July 1946, Mr C.F. Aeschlimann, who was the Chief ICRC Delegate in the SEAC area, was in company with Mr H. Pfrunder, who was the Assistant ICRC Delegate for Malaya, when he paid a visit to a repatriation vessel which was waiting to leave from the Selatar Naval Base in northern Singapore. The ship in question was the Liberty ship the *Sara Bache* that was waiting to leave for Otake in Japan with a mixture of 2,455 Japanese sailors and 355 Army workers. During the war, the Naval base at Selatar was in the control and use of the Japanese Navy.

The journey from Singapore to Japan had been estimated by the ship's captain, Tasaka, that it would take fourteen days to complete. Like him, his crew were all Japanese nationals. How they viewed their passengers, in relation to them having surrendered rather than committing suicide, is not known.

Before it set sail, the two ICRC delegates visited the ship to speak with some of the men and check the standard of their accommodation. They spoke with the ship's master as well as Lieutenant Yamanaka, a liaison officer with the Japanese Naval Headquarters, who was of great assistance.

It was noted that each of the men had straw mattresses to sleep on and that there was enough room on the vessel for the number of men on board. Each of the men the ICRC representatives saw appeared to be in very good physical condition. The ship's doctor confirmed there were sufficient medications on board for the men's needs, and in the case of a medical emergency, one of the men on board the ship, who was one of those being repatriated, was also a naval doctor.

The only point of concern for the ICRC delegates was the heat in the holds, which was considerable, but the ship's captain informed them that the situation would probably improve once the ship was under-way and out at sea.

Overall, the two ICRC delegates felt that the conditions on board the ship were satisfactory enough for it to sail, which it did at just after 1600 hours that day. Most if not all of those on board just wanted to get back home as quickly as they could and be reunited with their families and loved ones and, if the truth be known, they wouldn't have really cared what condition the ship was in. The war had been over for nearly a year, which for some of the men would have meant they hadn't seen their families and homes for nearly five years.

On 31 July 1946, Mr Aeschlimann conducted a visit to both Ayabe HQ Camp as well as Arima Unit Camp, both of which formed part of Changi prison, which was now being used to accommodate surren-dered Japanese personnel. The camp was to be found, not surprisingly, in the Changi district of Singapore, and was attached to a hospital as well as a convalescent camp for Japanese military personnel.

On the day of Mr Aeschlimann's visit to the camp there was a con-ference taking place at the prison for Labour Unit commanders, which was being run by Lieutenant General Kinoshita. This was in relation to Japanese prisoners of war who were being used by the British author-ities to carry out manual work in and around Singapore while been held as prisoners of war.

Lieutenant General Kitsuju Ayabe was the commanding officer for Japanese Surrendered Personnel working parties in Singapore. Lieutenant General Hayashi Kinoshita had been the general officer commanding the 3rd Air Army in Singapore since 14 December 1943, so he knew the island very well.

During the visit, the ICRC delegates were accompanied by Colonel Yamamoto, who was an army doctor. The two camps had a total of 286 officers and 4,287 non-commissioned officers and other ranks.

The camps' hospital was notably busy with 360 patients and another 465 in the camps convalescent unit, but with 3 doctors and 65 other medical staff, it was well catered for. Of the hospital's patients, 125 were suffering with malaria, 33 with external injuries that weren't specified as to what they were, there were 33 cases of beriberi, and 35 with diseases of the respiratory organs.

The weekly list of rations available for each man was considerable, with eighteen items listed on it, including vegetables, tinned meat, sugar, cheese, fish and fruit. Despite this, Colonel Yamamoto enquired if it was possible to receive more fresh meat and vegetables for his men. He also asked about the possibility of receiving sports equipment and reading materials. These requests were forwarded on to the Japanese Red Cross.

The Japanese prisoners were used by the British authorities for general labouring purposes, such as road making, cable laying, weeding, transport and construction work at Changi airfield. The work generally lasted for eight to ten hours a day, with one day allowed off each week. They were not paid for any of the work that they did, nor were any cigarettes provided and there was no on-site canteen.

In line with the regulations of the Geneva convention, officers were not compelled to carry out any kind of manual work.

The camp was spread over several square miles and consisted of hutments which were roofed with either thatch or corrugated iron and had wooden floors. Each man had his own mattress which was laid out directly on the floor. At the time of the visit there was a drought which meant a shortage of water which would have been made worse by the climate and humidity at that time of the year in Singapore. It was noted that the washing facilities within the camp required some improvement although the latrines were adequate and clean.

Overall, it was considered by the ICRC delegates that conditions in the camp were satisfactory.

I noted when reading through this report that I had not seen any similar reports by the ICRC for wartime visits to Japanese camps holding British prisoners on the island. The conditions of the camps that Japanese prisoners lived in, the food that was provided to them and the treatment they received was so different and so much better than anything that they had provided to Allied prisoners of war in the same camps.

Two days later, on 2 August 1946, Mr Aeschlimann visited Keppel Road Camp in Singapore. On this occasion he was on his own. He was accompanied throughout his visit by the commanding Japanese officer in the camp, Major Hanahoka and the senior medical officer, Captain Yasuda.

Including two doctors and five other medical staff, there were 1,241 prisoners in the camp, although for official reasons they were referred to as Japanese Surrendered Personnel.

The accommodation was a combination of hutments and tents, with the hutments having been built by the Japanese prisoners during their incarceration.

The food rations were the same as in other similar camps in Singapore, and on the day of Mr Aeschlimann's visit, the menu for the day was as follows:

Breakfast: Biscuits, potatoes, corned beef and cabbage.

Lunch: The same as for breakfast but with scones instead of biscuits.

Dinner: Japanese rice, potatoes and cabbage soup.

In the circumstances that wasn't too bad a selection of one day's dietary intake, especially when most local civilians might not be so fortunate as to have one meal a day, let alone three.

In the camp's hospital wing there were twenty-five men being cared for, most of whom were suffering with malaria. It was noted that there were sufficient medicines to cover the men's needs when they were sick, but there was a need for some more surgical equipment, which was more as a precaution than a necessity.

Major Hanahoka informed Mr Aeschlimann that repatriation for him and his men was, not surprisingly, of the utmost importance to them all, and was their main driving force. When Mr Aeschlimann politely suggested supplying the men with some games that they could play, Major Hanahoka replied that the work that his men had to undertake was very strenuous and left them feeling too tired to indulge in any kind of sporting or recreational pastime. All they did on their day off was sleep and do their personal washing.

Captain Yasuda asked for more room in the hospital wing, and was of the opinion that more of their men required hospital treatment than had actually come forward. Why he felt that wasn't clarified, nor were the ailments or illnesses from which he felt they might be suffering.

Mr Aeschlimann made comment that the Keppel Road camp was of a good standard, but added that he believed the men's morale was beginning to deteriorate, possibly because of their strong desire to be repatriated back home to their families in Japan, coupled with the frustration of not knowing when that was likely to be.

On the same day, he visited the Tanjong Pagar camp, which was located near the Singapore docks. The camp held a total of 2,664 Japanese military personnel and attached civilians. Ironically, during the Japanese occupation of the island it had been a prisoner of war camp which catered for Australian and British servicemen. Unlike when it was run by the Japanese during the war, Mr Aeschlimann reported that there was no overcrowding, with 150 men being housed in each of 18 barrack blocks. Rations for each of the prisoners were recorded as being more than sufficient. Most of the prisoners worked at the nearby Singapore docks, involved in loading and unloading commercial shipping.

There was a camp for Japanese Surrendered Personnel in the vicinity of the airfield at Sembawang, which was some eighteen kilometres north of Singapore city. Mr Aeschlimann visited the camp on 28 August 1946. It contained a total of 476 naval personnel of different ranks.

The camp was tented. Twenty-six men were allocated to each of the large tents, where the men slept on rush-made mats; officers had the slightly more comfortable experience of a bed. Most of the men were employed working at the nearby Sembawang airfield, while others were used to rebuild some of the city's roads.

Overall, conditions in the camp were so good that Mr Aeschlimann described Sembawang as the best prisoner of war camp in the whole of Singapore.

Mr Aeschlimann kept himself extremely busy in his role for the ICRC and in doing so displayed his organisation's unbiased approach to its work. Even on days of national and international celebrations Mr Aeschlimann didn't balk at his commitments. On 31 December 1946 he visited the Kluang Surrendered Personnel labour camp, which in effect comprised four separate camps. These were Headquarters Kluang, 34th Battalion, 143rd Battalion, and the 5th Artisan Company; but his subsequent report only covered the second and third camps which were located immediately next to Kluang airfield (34th Battalion) and on a little hill just north of Kluang (143rd Battalion) and between them they catered for 1,135 men.

The Japanese commanding officer for the camps was Major Emi. The 618 men of the 34th Battalion slept in tents, which had most definitely seen better days, while the 517 men of the 143rd Battalion slept in wooden huts, the roofs of which were in dire need of repair. The urinals and latrines in both camps were recorded as being in an adequate state of repair.

The food rations were the same for the prisoners as they were in other similar camps around Singapore, although there had been no fresh fruit or vegetables provided for the previous two months. But to help the men celebrate the New Year, they were each given ten ounces of fresh fruit and had been allowed to save up their weekly allowances of tapioca, and on the very day of Mr Aeschlimann's visit, the men were in the process of making cakes for the New Year.

Healthwise, the camp had quite a good record, with only sixty-four of the men recorded as being on the sick list; of these thirteen had contracted malaria.

Each man was provided with ten ounces of soap every month, which had been the case since September 1946. They were also, as from the very next day, each provided with twenty cigarettes a week. And roughly fifty per cent of the men from the 34th Battalion had received mail of some kind from loved ones back home. When the men received those letters, one wonders if they did so with some feelings of trepidation, not knowing how they would be treated by their families for having surrendered, even though they had been ordered to do so by their Emperor.

Under the heading of 'Requests and Complaints', Mr Aeschlimann had noted that thirty of the men from one of the camps, who were all from the city of Okinawa, had asked for their repatriation back to Japan to be made a priority, but there was no specific reason as to why the request had been made.

It was also noted that there was a distinct lack of games and sports equipment available for the men and that a supply of fresh fruit and vegetables was also needed. These requests and complaints appeared to be somewhat generic within most of the camps.

There was also a heading in the report covering 'General Remarks'. These were not complaints from any of the camps' Japanese soldiers, or disparaging remarks made by Mr Aeschlimann, but simply observations which he had made. He had made note of the fact that in the camp of the men from the 143rd Battalion there were fifty men who were aged 40 or above. The issue of pay had also been raised, but the report wasn't clear whether that meant the prisoners weren't actually paid, or wanted a pay rise on what they already earned. There was also a point made about sending financial allowances to their dependants back home in Japan. One would assume that even though they were prisoners in a foreign country, they would still be receiving their pay as soldiers.

Mr Aeschlimann's final comment was that the men from the camp who were being used as labourers were receiving insufficient food rations to allow for the level of physical work they were being requested to undertake. It is notable that in all of the reports concerning visits to the camps which held 'Japanese Surrendered Personnel' in Singapore, all of the visits were carried out by Mr Aeschlimann and not Mr Schweizer, who had been the wartime ICRC delegate for the island of Singapore.

Mr Aeschlimann visited the Miura Unit in the Jurong district of Singapore on 9 August 1946. It was a relatively big camp, covering an area of 160 acres, located nine miles north of Singapore City in hilly woodland which had previously been a car park. In total it catered for 1,313 officers, men and civilians. The camp's commanding Japanese officer was Naval Commander Miura – there seemed to be a habit of naming a camp after the commanding officer. The senior medical officer was Lieutenant Kichire Masegi. The men lived in ten wooden hutments which had wooden floors and thatched roofs. They slept on traditional Japanese tatamis, which were made out of rice straw with a covering of woven soft rush straw. A tatami is exactly twice the length of its width.

The camp had four cookhouses and a staggering twenty-four cooks to feed the officers and men. Like all of the other camps there was a varied and plentiful diet, with fresh vegetables being delivered to the camp on average three times a week. To supplement this, a vegetable garden had been started by the inmates within the camp, where the intention was mainly to grow Kang Kong, which is a tropical type of spinach.

The camp's menu on the day of the visit by Mr Aeschlimann was:

Breakfast: A pudding made of rice, corned beef, and vegetables.

Lunch: Biscuits, Japanese tea.

Dinner: Same as for breakfast plus milk tea.

The camp had its own hospital wing with four doctors and eighteen medical orderlies, and on the day of the visit there were thirty-nine patients being treated, the main ailment, once again being Malaria. The hospital was quite roomy, and not surprisingly it was noted as being very clean. There was a shortage of bandages and disinfectants.

Both Commander Miura and Doctor Masegi complained that quite often patients who they have sent to Nee Soon hospital on the island for more intensive treatment, are returned to them still not properly recovered and certainly not fit or well enough to go back to work.

Most of the camp's men, over 1,100 of them in total, did heavy manual work in either Ordnance Depots or Petrol Dumps. The upside of this was that because of this the entire camp benefitted by receiving fifty per cent more in their daily rations, the downside was that despite their hard work and long hours, on average ten hours per day, they were not paid and no cigarettes had been provided for over five months.

Most if not all of the men were desperately waiting to receive letters from their loved ones back home in Japan, but only a small number of the men had actually received any correspondence. This was nothing to do with the British authorities or the Red Cross, it was simply down to logistics, where placing civilian structures back in to everyday life after four years of war took time, especially back in Japan, that was still slowly recovering from the atomic bombs dropped on Hiroshima and Nagasaki.

The camp was guarded by a detachment of fifty Indian soldiers. The ICRC report doesn't expand on the point by way of an explanation as to why this was necessary. It wouldn't have been to do with anybody in the camp being suspected of war crimes, because all such enemy combatants were locked up in Changi prison while they awaited trial.

Woodlands Japanese Surrendered Personnel Camp had first been visited by Mr C F Aeschlimann on 8 August 1946, he visited it again, nearly a year later, on 10 June 1947. He was greeted by the Japanese Commanding officer in the camp, Captain Taro Taguchi, who during the war had been a Chief of Staff in the 3rd Air Fleet, who were charged with the air defence of Eastern Japan.

The main topic of conversation between the two men was the issue of repatriation. Captain Taguchi's men were understandably becoming somewhat frustrated and restless, as to the reasons why they were not being allowed to return home to Japan. None of them were suspected war criminals, and the war had been over for nearly two years. The main reason for their frustration was because nobody was telling them anything about their situation. Receiving their pay more expediently and rubber boots, for those who were assigned to clean out septic tanks at Nee Soon British camp, were other points raised by Captain Taguchi.

Woodlands was in fact made up of four smaller sub camps. Mr C F Aeschlimann reported that conditions in the camp were quite satisfactory, with the men living in either hutments or tents. They were all receiving a varied and ample diet and there were sufficient sporting activities for the men to take part in, along with a theatre and educational centres, although it is not clear on what topic the men were receiving education on.

The biggest cause of sickness in the camp, wasn't malaria as it was in most other camps, but nothing more serious than the common cold, closely followed by minor accidents which in the main came about as a result of their outside work.

Collectively, the four camps had a total of 478 men showing as being in hospital on the day of Mr C F Aeschlimann's visit, a further 109 men were sick and awaiting their repatriation to Japan. These were men who had already been informed that they were to be repatriated and were simply waiting to leave.

On 22 August 1946 Mr C F Aeschlimann, visited the Arima Unit Camp at Changi for a second time having previously carried out a visit there, less than a month before on 31 July 1946. This time he was met by the camp's Japanese Commanding officer, Colonel Arima and senior medical officer, Lieutenant Saito.

Mr C F Aeschlimann visited Semba Wang camp, which is situated close to Sembawang airfield, which is north of Singapore City, on 29 August 1946. It was regarded as the best Japanese Surrendered Personnel Camp in the whole of Singapore, where discipline was of a very high standard.

He was met by and escorted on his visit of the camp, by the Japanese Commanding Officer, Lieutenant Akimatsu, and the senior medical officer Lieutenant A Oshio.

There were a total of 476 men in the camp, all of whom belonged to the Imperial Japanese Navy. At the time of the visit, seventeen of the men were in hospital with malaria, influenza, beri-beri, external complaints and five who had internal complaints. There were also a further fourteen men who were recorded as being on light duties.

The accommodation was nice and comfortable and consisted of twenty-six large tents, which each slept twenty-six men, who slept on rush mats which were laid out on the floor. Officers also slept in tents, but they had the added luxury of sleeping on comfortable beds which were raised off of the ground. The hospital accommodation consisted of mattresses laid out on raised wooden platforms, each of which was surrounded by a mosquito net.

A lot of the men in the camp had decided that they would like to learn English, so a 'school' had been set up in one of the large tents, it also doubled as a reading room when not being used as a classroom.

The men from Sembawang all worked at either the nearby Sembawang airfield or on road building projects.

On 9 January 1947, Mr C F Aeschlimann, once again visited the Nee Soon Japanese hospital in Singapore, having previously visited there five months earlier on 16 August 1946. He was met by the Japanese officer commanding, Major-General K Hosoya.

In between the dates of the two visits, some 443 men had left the hospital and been repatriated back home to Japan. Just two days earlier on 7 January 1947, 406 men, which included 40 who were suffering with TB, had left for Japan on the hospital ship, the SS *Oxfordshire*. On the same day 137 men, most of whom were walking cases, had left for Japan on board the SS *Choran Maru*.

This exodus had left a lot of room at the hospital, which was good for the other Japanese soldiers who were still there. Besides providing them with more space it also left more staff who were able to look after them.

In his previous visit Mr Aeschlimann had recorded the bad state of the roofs on some of the men's hutments, which was where they slept. He was glad to see that his comments and observations about their condition had solicited an expedient response. Most of the roofs had been repaired, but by the use of tarpaulins as at the time there was a shortage of useable wood throughout Singapore.

The levels of food rationing had sustained which allowed the men to continue with a varied and nutritional diet. The menu of the day was posted on the hospital's notice board, which was as follows:

Breakfast: Biscuits and tinned herring.

Lunch: Rice mixed with sweet potato. Potato soup containing sweet potato, carrot and mutton.

Dinner: Rice mixed with potato and carrot. Soup containing salmon, carrot and Kangkong.

Nearly 60 per cent of the hospital's patients were on increased diets to help assist with their recovery programmes, particularly the fever cases.

Originally the hospital had been connected to the nearby mental hospital in Yio Chyu Kiang Road, but in July the same year, the two hospitals had gone their own separate ways allowing the Nee Soon hospital to carry on caring for soldiers from the numerous Japanese Surrendered Personnel camps that were located throughout the island, as well as those from neighbouring Malaya, Siam, Burma, and Sumatra. Having fully recovered they would then be repatriated back to Japan. Having fewer patients to deal with meant that they could also allocate some of their medical supplies to the Japanese Surrendered Personnel camps, for the doctors there to be able to deal with more of the less urgent cases, meaning less patients that had to be sent to them in the first place. Nee Soon Japanese hospital carried a staff of 247 in total which included 15 doctors and 2 dentists.

Since the date of the Japanese capitulation and up to the date of the visit, the hospital had treated a total of 16,790 Japanese military personnel, 203 of whom had subsequently died as a result of their wounds, illnesses or diseases. A further 8,025 had already been repatriated back to Japan.

On the day of the visit by Mr Aeschlimann, he noted that there were a total of 752 patients being treated at the hospital, this included 90 cases of pulmonary infiltration, which included TB, 48 who were suffering with beri-beri, 31 with malaria, 54 who were wounded, who must have been bad, as the war had been over for more than a year, although this also included those who were injured on working party details or in motor vehicle related accidents. There were even 17 who had venereal diseases, which threw up the obvious question as to how Japanese soldiers who were detained in camps in areas which had been occupied by Japanese forces during the war, could possibly manage to find anybody prepared to have sex with them.

The report, although generally favourable in relation to the facilities in place and the assistance that had been provided by the British authorities, also included the suggestion that some of the periodic overcrowding, along with the injuries, deaths and diseases, was directly connected to the work which the Japanese soldiers were being allocated, such as heavy labour type work and the cleaning the city's drains.

The very last page of the report contained a petition from Major-General Hosoya to the ICRC via Mr Aeschlimann.

*'We should like to have the same treatment for our patients as British patients receive. If it is impossible for our patients to receive this treatment, the hospital expects the medical service of the Japanese Red Cross from Japan to be invited to replace it.*

*The issue of money has been prohibited to us since we are surrendered personnel. The organization of this hospital is quite different from others, although everything is managed by the British authorities. We find inconveniences when urgent items are required. For instance, the purchasing of special drugs, the obtaining of repairing and constructing materials and of ice for patients with high fever. We desire an expenditure for fresh fruits, meat, vegetables and special diets, and necessities for the more serious cases. Funeral expenditure is needed and a well-nourished diet for blood donors. We also require hair dressing instruments and amusements.*

*We would like to have a replacement of mattresses, sheets and sleeping suits for the serious cases. Those being used are gradually damaged and much soiled.*

*We wonder whether we could be supplied with a special patients' diet of 100 per cent instead of 60 per cent of the patients' strength. It would be highly appreciated if eggs, fresh meat, fresh fruits, butter and other seasonings could be issued for 15 per cent of the very serious cases.*

*We would like to have damaged structures repaired completely. We should be really pleased if we could have a supply of medical books in Japanese or in English on various treatments.'*

I found Major-General Hosoya's petition to the ICRC extremely intriguing. There is a very subtle difference between Japanese Surrendered Personnel and Allied Prisoners of War. All Japanese military personnel were ordered to lay down their weapons and cease all hostilities, an order given to them by their Emperor, which they had to obey, although some who saw surrender in any form as being a dishonour that they could not live with, chose to commit suicide. While fighting they killed at will, even unarmed wounded combatants, some lying in hospital beds were shown no mercy or honour, as they were barbarically despatched to the afterlife. To them enemy soldiers who surrendered had no honour and had given up the right to expect to be treated with any respect or dignity. This was often given as the reason or justification for their treatment of Allied prisoners of war who they brutalised and murdered. Civilians were treated no differently and sometimes, much worst.

As we have also seen there were occasions when Allied soldiers fought extremely bravely and only gave up the fight when they had run out of ammunition or had been wounded, but still the Japanese did not treat them honourably or with any respect. They killed them, sometimes in the most brutal way possible.

It is only right to balance this account, as not all Japanese officers and soldiers conducted themselves in this manner, and it would be wrong to suggest that they did.

When Singapore was surrendered to the Japanese, Allied soldiers were ordered by their senior officers to lay down their arms and surrender themselves to the Japanese, this they did, but they weren't called Allied Surrendered Personnel, they were classified as Prisoners of War and in lots of cases treated appallingly. With this in mind, I couldn't help but think how the British officer who ended up reading that report from the International Committee of the Red Cross, which included the petition from Major-General Hosoya, felt once he had fully digested its contents, with the knowledge of how British and Allied prisoners of war had been treated by the Japanese.

I believe that initially there would have been an element of shock and maybe even utter disbelief at what he was reading, but ultimately he would have remained calm and professional, and did whatever it was within his power to do in the circumstances.

# CHAPTER TWENTY FOUR

# REPARATIONS AND APOLOGY

I will start this chapter looking at the issue of war reparations in general before localising it to Singapore's situation as a result of Japan's occupation of the country between February 1942 and September 1945.

What are war reparations? They usually come in the form of a monetary compensation to cover the costs of damage or injury that the losing nation in a war is forced to agree to pay to the victorious nations. As of January 2015, Japan has stated that the only nation she still has any outstanding issues with in relation to war reparations is South Korea.

The main problem with war reparations is the negative economic affect that they have on the general population of the vanquished nation and not on those who waged the war in the first place. The country's leaders and military personnel were the ones who put their country on a war footing in the first place without any say or influence in the matter from the people, but with the implementation of war reparations it is the general populace of the defeated nation who ultimately suffer.

If the war reparations that are imposed on a losing nation are too draconian, all they achieve is to push that nation into a deeper and deeper economic nightmare from which they can see no way out; this makes it highly unlikely that the enforced repayments will be made. It can also lead to a rise in nationalistic elements, like a phoenix rising from the ashes of what was once their great nation, then to become a rampant breeding ground of resentment towards the victorious nation.

Many historians have given their support to the theory that the Second World War came about as a direct result of the extremely heavy war reparations placed upon Germany at the end of the First World War as part of the conditions of the Treaty of Versailles in 1919. It sowed the seeds of the Nazi Party and Adolph Hitler.

Some historians also suggest that the better way to deal with such situations is to place tough restrictions on all of the military wings of a belligerent nation, only allowing small numbers of personnel and placing restrictions on the numbers of ships, aircraft, tanks and artillery pieces they are allowed to have at any time, with strict measures in place to make sure the restrictions are adhered to.

How did Singapore fare in relation to receiving financial reparations from Japan? Well, to start with, at the time of the Second World War Singapore was not a sovereign nation in her own right, but a British colony. Japan had made reparations to Britain in different ways, one of which was to pay for certain crown buildings which had been damaged by the Japanese during the war; this was part of the San Francisco Treaty of 1951. It has to be remembered that a post-war Japan was being economically supported by America who was exerting pressure on her European allies not to burden Japan with even more claims for financial reparations. Not only was this the post-war era, but the beginning of the cold war, so there were now new problems for the world's leading powers to deal with and political favours were being called in.

Japan's future discussions with Singapore over reparations were effected accordingly and Japan's initial stance on the matter was that she had already made reparations, so she refused to either apologise or discuss any future war reparations.

But Singapore was not prepared to let the matter drop, and when she gained her full independence after she split with Malaysia on 9 August 1965, she tried once again, asking for both war reparations and an apology for the atrocities Japan had carried out across the island.

After some lengthy debate between the two nations, an agreement was finally struck on 25 October 1966, but only after continual disagreement over what it should be called. In the end Japan won the argument and the agreement was simply entitled 'the agreement between Japan and Singapore dated 25 October 1966'. Singapore was not entirely happy with the situation but understandably did not wish to risk coming out of the negotiations without anything at all because of a disagreement over what to call the agreement.

Japan never did make an apology for the atrocities and mass murders she committed during her three-and-a-half-year occupation of Singapore, but she did agree to pay $50 million in compensation, half of which was a grant, while the other half was in the shape of a loan.

They say that 'time is a great healer' and 'to move forward one has to let go of the past.' Sometimes the injury is so great that, no matter what, it will linger in the memory for evermore – but the word 'sorry' helps. Imagine how a people would feel if that was not forthcoming.

It is also about perception and interpretation many years later. On Thursday, 26 December 2013, the Japanese Prime Minister Shinzo Abe paid an early morning visit to the Yasukuni war shrine in Tokyo. Whether he had considered what the potential ramifications would be of that visit is not known, although I am sure that he had. Firstly, and to make sure I am not being presumptuous, let me explain what the Yasukuni war shrine is. It is a Shinto shrine which is located at Chiyoda, in Tokyo. It commemorates anyone who has died or been killed while in the service of the Empire of Japan, which existed from the time of Emperor Meiji all the way through until the nation was renamed during the Allied occupation in 1947. The shrine now lists the names of 2,466,532 men, women and children, including 1,068 who were found guilty and convicted at Allied war crimes trials; fourteen of these are 'A-Class', the worst possible kind. The shrine also commemorates anyone who died on behalf of the Empire, which is not only soldiers, but relief workers, factory workers, and other citizens, as well as those not born of Japanese ethnicity, such as Taiwanese and Koreans, but who served Japan during war time.

The shrine is visited by thousands of people each week from all over the country and from all different walks of life, who go there to be near to and to pray for the spirit of their loved ones who gave their lives for their Emperor. That is only to be expected, but when one of those people is the country's Prime Minister, it has a very different meaning.

Ironically one of the reasons he chose to visit the shrine when he did was because of the poor state of political relations between Japan and both China and South Korea. So badly taken was the visit by South Korea that its Vice Foreign Minister, Kim Kyou Hyun, visited the Deputy Chief of the Japanese embassy in Seoul, Takashi Kurai, to protest about Mr Abe's visit.

The date of Mr Abe's visit to the shrine was significant on a personal level as it was a year to the day that he had become Prime Minister. He told waiting reporters, who were there by invitation only, that the reason for the timing of his visit was so that he could 'report before the souls of the war dead how my administration has worked for one year,' also adding his renewed pledge that Japan would never go to war again. Besides the potential political ramifications of his visit, there was also the possible damage to Japanese companies such as the car manufacturers Nissan, Toyota and Honda and their business interests in China.

The response in Singapore came from the country's Minister of Foreign Affairs who said, 'such visits reopen old grievances, and are unhelpful to building trust and confidence in the region.'

Even America, a staunch ally of today's Japan, was unimpressed with Mr Abe's visit. They had tried right up until a few hours beforehand to get Mr Abe to cancel his visit, but to no avail. The Japanese media took a dim view too, turning on Mr Abe. There were demonstrations and the burning of placards outside the Japanese Embassy in Seoul.

All of that goes to show that seventy-one years after Japan invaded Singapore, emotions still linger long in the memory about what happened all those years ago, and how one ill-thought-out decision by such a prominent and high profile individual can have such a wide-reaching and negative effect on both political and hard-earned business relationships in the region.

# CHAPTER TWENTY FIVE

# KRANJI WAR CEMETERY

The Kranji war cemetery is situated some twenty-two kilometres north of the city of Singapore and overlooks the Straits of Johore. It contains the graves of 4,461 British and other Commonwealth service men of the Second World War who were killed during fighting either in the Battle of Singapore or who died during the Japanese occupation of the island. Sadly, 850 of those buried there remain unidentified.

Prior to 1939, the Kranji area had been a military camp, but by the time Japan had begun her invasion of Malaya it had become a large ammunition dump for British forces based on the island of Singapore. After racing down the Malay Peninsula in double quick time, Japanese forces crossed the Johore Straits on 8 February 1942, landing at the mouth of the River Kranji, less than two miles away from where the cemetery is today. There then followed three days of some extremely fierce fighting on both sides, which on occasions was so brutal and at such close quarters that it was down to hand-to-hand combat. The fighting only came to a halt when Australian forces felt compelled to withdraw from their position due to the superior size of the Japanese forces they were up against, as well as their overwhelming air support.

After the British had surrendered Singapore, the Japanese turned the area at Kranji into a prisoner of war camp for Commonwealth servicemen who had come under their control.

With Japan's surrender after the dropping of the two atom bombs on 6 and 9 August 1945, at Hiroshima and Nagasaki, and the reoccupation of Singapore by Commonwealth forces, the small cemetery at Kranji, which had been started by the camp's prisoners, became more of a permanent location with the help and assistance of the Army Graves Service.

During the war the largest prisoner of war camp on the island was the one at Changi. There was also another prisoner of war camp at Buona Vista. The graves at these locations were removed and taken to Kranji, where they were reburied.

The cemetery at Kranji also contains a memorial to a group of sixty-nine Chinese servicemen, who were all members of the

Commonwealth forces when they were killed by the Japanese during the time of their occupation of Singapore.

The **Singapore Memorial**, which commemorates the names of 24,000 Commonwealth servicemen, is contained within the Kranji War Cemetery. Those commemorated on the memorial all died during the campaigns in Malaya and Indonesia or while being held in captivity as prisoners of war. Many of these individuals have no known date of death and in these instances the date when they went missing or were captured has been used instead.

The **Singapore (Unmaintainable Graves) Memorial**, which also stands within the cemetery, commemorates the names of some 250 Commonwealth servicemen who died as a result of the fighting in either Malaya or Singapore. These men all have known graves in civilian cemeteries, but for religious reasons it was not possible to have their remains removed and reburied at Kranji.

The **Singapore Cremation Memorial** commemorates the names of nearly 800 servicemen, mostly who were serving with Indian Regiments; in keeping with their religious beliefs, they were cremated as soon as was possible after their deaths.

The **Singapore Civil Hospital Grave Memorial** commemorates some 400 servicemen and civilians who were buried in what had originally been dug as an emergency water tank in the grounds of one of Singapore's hospitals.

The reason for the need of a mass grave was the sheer number of wounded who had arrived at the hospital in such a short time frame and who had subsequently died of their wounds. This in turn made the task of individual burials in the normal manner an impossible task. After the reoccupation of Singapore by Commonwealth forces at the end of the Second World War, the matter was looked at once again. It was decided that individual identification of any of the deceased would by now be impossible, and accordingly the mass grave should remain undisturbed. It was suitably tidied up and the ground in which it lay was consecrated by the Bishop of Singapore. A cross commemorating all of those buried there was erected over the grave by the military authorities.

As has already been mentioned in this chapter, there are a total of 4,461 Commonwealth servicemen buried at the Kranji War Cemetery. I thought it might be useful to provide a breakdown of how many men died on each day beginning with 8 February 1942 and continuing through until 24 February 1942.

On the evening of 8 February 1942, elements of the 5th and 18th Army divisions of the Imperial Japanese Army crossed the narrow Johore Straits, which separate the island of Singapore from mainland Malaya, in some fifty small boats. By the following morning thousands of Japanese troops had landed on Singapore and the final battle for the capture of the island was underway.

The figures I have used are based on information available on the Commonwealth War Graves Commission website. The numbers show the total that died or were killed in February 1942:

| | |
|---|---|
| 8 February: | 42 |
| 9 February: | 147 |
| 10 February: | 107 |
| 11 February: | 127 |
| 12 February: | 48 |
| 13 February: | 92 |
| 14 February: | 139 |
| 15 February: | 193 |
| 16 February: | 11 |
| 17 February: | 17 |
| 18 February: | 13 |
| 19 February: | 9 |
| 20 February: | 16 |
| 21 February: | 12 |
| 22 February: | 11 |
| 23 February: | 7 |

The next day, 24 February 1942, was the first day since the surrender of Singapore that no Commonwealth servicemen had died or been killed since the beginning of the Battle of Singapore. This does not include figures for civilian losses during the same time frame.

From looking at the figures it is clear to see that the two days with the heaviest loss of life were the first full day of the battle, when 147 Commonwealth servicemen died or were killed, and the last day, when 193 lost their lives.

I thought it would be interesting to look at the different Commonwealth regiments who lost men during and in the immediate aftermath of the Battle of Singapore. The regiments are shown in alphabetical order. When it has not been possible to identify the relevant battalion, the regiment's name is recorded on its own.

Argyll & Sutherland Highlanders.
Army Dental Corps.
Army Educational Corps.
Australian Army Medical Corps.
Australian Army Ordnance Corps.
Australian Army Postal Service.
Australian Army Provost Corps.
Australian Infantry, 2nd/18th and 2nd/19th Battalions.
Australian Corps of Signals.
(10th) Baluch Regiment, 2nd Battalion.
Bedfordshire & Hertfordshire Regiment, 5th Battalion.
Cambridgeshire Regiment, 2nd Battalion.
Chinese Labour Corps, Malay Forces.
Dalforce.
(17th) Dogra Regiment, 3rd Battalion.
East Surrey Regiment, 2nd Battalion.
Federated Malay States Volunteer Force.
Gordon Highlanders, 2nd Battalion.
Hong Kong & Singapore Royal Artillery.
Hyderabad Infantry, Indian State Force, 1st Battalion.
Indian Armoured Corps, 100th Light Tank Squadron.
Indian Army Ordnance Corps.
Indian General Service Corps.
Indian Medical Department.
Leicestershire Regiment, 1st Battalion.
Malay Regiment.
Manchester Regiment.
Merchant Navy.
(1st) Punjab Regiment, 6th Battalion.
(14th) Punjab Regiment, 6th Battalion.
(16th) Punjab Regiment, 2nd Battalion.
Reconnaissance Corps, 18th Regiment
Royal Air Force.
Royal Army Chaplains Department.
Royal Army Medical Corps.
Royal Army Ordnance Corps, 18th Ordnance Workshop.
Royal Army Service Corps.
Royal Artillery.

Royal Australian Air Force.
Royal Australian Artillery.
Royal Australian Engineers.
Royal Corps of Signals.
Royal Engineers, 287th Field Company.
Royal Norfolk Regiment, 6th Battalion.
Royal Northumberland Fusiliers, 9th Battalion.
Sherwood Foresters (Notts & Derby Regiment), 1st/5th Battalion.
Straits Settlements Volunteer Force.
Suffolk Regiment, 4th & 5th Battalions.
The Loyal Regiment (North Lancashire)
Voluntary Aid Detachment.
'Z' Force Special Unit.

All of the above do not of course include those who were killed at sea during the same period of time. This would include the Australian Army Nurses who were killed and murdered as a result of the sinking of the Sarawak Royal Yacht *Vyner Brooke* and the subsequent massacre at Bangka Island. Their names are however included on the Kranji War Memorial.

Remarkably, there are fifty-one separate British and Commonwealth regiments, corps, or other units that lost personnel as a result of trying to defend Singapore against the invading Japanese forces.

# CHAPTER TWENTY SIX

# BRITISH WAR CABINET MEETINGS

Records of the War Cabinet Meetings supplied me with some very useful snippets of information about the changing situation in Singapore throughout the war.

The following meeting took place at Richmond Terrace, London, SW1:

### 18 March 1940
### Withdrawal of Two RAF Bomber Squadrons from Singapore to India
### Memorandum by the Chiefs of Staff Committee

(1) *The War Cabinet will recall that on the outbreak of war that part of the air plan for the reinforcement of Singapore which related to the despatch from India of two medium bomber squadrons was put into operation. This was intended as an insurance against the possibility of Japanese hostility.*

(2) *Since [then] the situation has changed materially in that the risk of war with Japan has considerably receded, while that of war with Russia has increased, with the resulting implications on the situation in India and the Middle East.*

(3) *We consider therefore, that the time has come when the two Blenheim squadrons sent from India last September should be recalled to India, where they would be more suitably placed either to reinforce Iraq or Egypt or to act as a counter to Russian air action against Northern India. They could of course, if the situation at Singapore suddenly deteriorated, rapidly be sent back there if the balance of risk so required.*

(4) *In recommending the above measure, we do not wish to give the impression that there can be a general relaxation of our precautionary measures in the Far East. The withdrawal of these squadrons throws an additional responsibility on the remainder of the garrison of Singapore, and makes it all the more important*

*that all units should be alert and efficient. This aspect of the
matter has been under consideration by the Overseas Defence
Committee, and we understand that a communication is about
to be addressed to the Governor of the Straits Settlements, urg-
ing him to take such measures as may be practicable, without
thereby causing dislocation of the vital tin and rubber industries, to extend training of the Volunteer units. In this way it
may be possible to correct any false impression which would
otherwise be caused by the move of these squadrons.*

| | |
|---|---|
| *Signed* | *C L N Newall* |
| *Signed* | *Dudley Pound* |
| *Signed* | *Edmund Ironside* |

It was interesting to note that in March 1940 there appeared to be
absolutely no chance of war between Britain and Japan, to such a
degree of certainty that the British authorities were more than happy
to move two medium bomber squadrons from Singapore to India.

The very next day, 19 March 1940, the memorandum that had been
set out by the chiefs of staff concerning the reduction in the number
of bomber squadrons to be held at Singapore went before the full War
Cabinet Committee:

*The Chief of the Air Staff explained the main points in the
Memorandum and gave particulars of the air forces which would
remain at Singapore after this withdrawal.*

*In reply to a question by the First Lord of the Admiralty, he said
that he thought it would be possible to leave some at least of the
spares at Singapore, as these could, if necessary, be used for the 2
Blenheim squadrons which would remain at Singapore. The aircraft
and their crews would fly to India, but the rest of the personnel of
the squadrons would go by sea. If, later, it was necessary to reinforce
Singapore, the aircraft could be flown back from India, and the men
could follow by sea in about a week.*

*The Lord Privy Seal suggested that by way of reassuring public
opinion in the Straits Settlements, prominence should be given, at
the time of their withdrawal, to the fact that these squadrons could be
very quickly brought back from India.*

*The Secretary of State for Dominion Affairs referred to the
interest which was taken by Australia and New Zealand in the
defence of Singapore. He recalled that, at our request, 5 destroyers*

*of the Australian Navy had, with the consent of the Australian Government, been sent from Singapore to the Mediterranean. He therefore suggested that it would be both politic and courteous that we should consult the Australian and New Zealand Governments before actually withdrawing the 2 Bomber squadrons. This would take only 2 or 3 days, and he had no doubt they would agree.*

*The War Cabinet –*

*Approved the withdrawal of 2 Bomber Squadrons from Singapore to India subject to the condition that this move should not be carried out until the Secretary of State for Dominion Affairs had consulted the Governments of Australia and New Zealand and obtained their concurrence in this step.*

This was no longer just about the potential threat to Malaya and Singapore, as well as the other nations in the immediate vicinity, but if Singapore in particular fell, then this also placed the west coast of Australia at the mercy of the advancing Japanese military might, and from there it would be like a house of cards as country after country became part of their new Pacific and South East Asia Empire.

On 25 May 1940, point twelve on the agenda was as follows:

*(12) The retention of Singapore is very important for economic control, particularly of rubber and tin. To counter Japanese action in the Far East, a fleet, adequately supported by air forces, is necessary at Singapore. It is most improbable that we could send naval forces there, and reliance would have to be placed upon the United States to safeguard our interests.*

It struck me from reading these minutes that there was no mention or concern about the local indigenous populations and the responsibility that Britain had to the people of Singapore, which after all was an island under British rule and protection governed by British laws. The only interest and worry shown was for the safeguarding of the natural resources of tin and rubber.

The theme of the United States of America playing their part in the Far East continued in further discussions of the British War Cabinet. The aide memoire, which covered ten separate points, was intended for the British Ambassador in Washington and outlined exactly what it was that the British Government expected from her American allies:

## 13 June 1940
## War Cabinet
## Plans to meet a Certain Eventuality
## Memoire by the Chiefs of Staff Committee.

### *Point (8). Far East.*

*The collapse of France would provide Japan with the temptation to take action against French, Dutch or British interests in the Far East. We see no hope of being able to despatch a fleet to Singapore. It will therefore be vital that the United States of America should publicly declare her intention to regard any alteration of the status quo in the Far East as a casus belli.*

Taking into account that this was June 1940 and the simultaneous attacks on Pearl Harbor, Hong Kong and Thailand wouldn't happen for another eighteen months, this would have given Britain plenty of time to get a fleet together and arrive in Singapore with more than enough time to spare.

The minutes of the meeting of 29 June 1940, Policy in the Far East, Memorandum by the Secretary of State for Foreign Affairs, were stamped:

### TO BE KEPT UNDER LOCK AND KEY
### It is requested that special care may be taken to ensure
### the secrecy of this document.

It is a very interesting document. It began with talk about wanting to avoid trouble with Japan while at the same time understanding that the making of any concessions would not necessarily improve relations between Britain and Japan. While deciding how to best placate Japan, Britain also had to be mindful not to make a decision which could in turn damage confidence in her policy in both China and the United States of America.

Japan had placed certain demands on Britain in relation to her presence in certain areas of the Far East. One such demand was for Britain to remove her troops and warships from areas of China that Japan occupied. The demands didn't stop there. She also wanted Britain to stop supplying the Chinese Government with war materials and supplies via Hong Kong and Burma, which included arms, ammunitions, oil, gasoline and lorries.

Initially these demands had been made in a somewhat menacing fashion by the Director of Military Intelligence of the Japanese General

Staff to the British Military Attaché in Tokyo. They were later toned down somewhat when they were confirmed in politer diplomatic language by the Japanese Minister of Foreign Affairs to His Majesty's Ambassador in Tokyo.

Before making any decisions on whether or not she would withdraw her troops from her garrisons in China or choose to retain them, the British Government had to contend with the knowledge that the United States Government had informed Japan that they would only offer diplomatic assistance to China and not armed support.

The issue as to whether to agree to the Japanese demand of closing the Burma Road supply route into China was a major one which had far-reaching implications. If Britain gave in to the Japanese, it would effectively send a message to China that Britain didn't care about her or what happened to her. There was the added issue of what message it would send out to the Americans, who were sympathetic to the countries of the Far East.

There was discussion on the point of acceding to the Japanese request as a means of ensuring that they stayed out of the European war, even though there was no guarantee that the Japanese would agree to this. Britain's ambassador in Tokyo was seriously concerned that to give way on this matter would be seen by the Japanese as a weakness which would simply lead to them making more and more demands as time went on.

One of the more important issues as far as Japan was concerned was Britain's military garrisons which she had located in Shanghai, Peking and Tientsin, although both of the latter had been greatly reduced in numbers from the start of the Second World War.

To reduce the numbers of troops at the Shanghai garrison would not have been appreciated by the Chinese Government, its very existence seen as a commitment by Britain to help defend China from the Japanese. A complete withdrawal of the military garrisons would result in a serious loss of prestige and respect for Britain. She would be totally capitulating to the Japanese in the hope, very possibly misplaced, that they would stay out of the European war.

It was amazing to think that the British Government were prepared to acquiesce to the Japanese over the issues of their military garrisons in China, regardless of the damage that would be caused to her relations with China as well as the United States of America, simply so as not to provoke the Japanese.

At 11 am on Wednesday, 4 September 1940, there was a meeting of the War Cabinet at number 10 Downing Street in London. The agenda had eight items for discussion including the French colonies, aircraft production, India, harvest work, the colonies, the Balkans and the Far East.

It was obvious from the tone of the discussion that the British Government Ministers were deeply afraid of becoming embroiled in a war with Japan. The minutes of the meeting read like a game of political cat and mouse, with those sitting round the table trying to work out how far they could push the Japanese without it resulting in all-out war, while balancing how much they could concede without appearing to be too weak. Economic inducements were even considered as a means of appeasing the Japanese. They knew that fighting a war on two fronts had to be avoided at all costs if possible. Nevertheless, they knew full well that war with Japan was very likely to happen eventually.

With matters as they were throughout Europe and the worry that Germany would invade Britain, home defence was clearly the priority.

Britain was also hoping that the United States of America would come to her rescue in relation to the threat posed by Japan in the Pacific and the Far East, but with America already refusing to become embroiled in the war in Europe, the chances of her throwing herself into a war with Japan, unless she had no other choice, were extremely slim.

By 10 November 1940 Japan's open and continued aggression towards China was becoming a real issue. At a meeting of the British War Cabinet on that day at 10 Downing Street, the Secretary of State for Foreign Affairs produced a memorandum for discussion. The Chinese General, Chiang Kai-Shek, had approached the British Ambassador in Chungking requesting closer Anglo-Chinese-American cooperation and financial loans of between £50 and £75 million. The request for help also included up to 1,000 aircraft per annum and a commitment from the Chinese that if Britain and America became involved in a war with Japan, the Chinese Army would also participate, and all Chinese aerodromes would be placed at the disposal of the Allied forces.

## 5pm Monday 24 February 1941 at 10 Downing Street, London, War Cabinet Meeting

*The Prime Minister reported that he had had an interview with the Japanese Ambassador in London. The Ambassador had said that his country had no aggressive intentions against Australia, Singapore or the Netherlands East Indies. He had handed the Ambassador a*

*Memorandum in reply to the message from the Japanese Minister for Foreign Affairs to Mr Eden.*

*Sir Robert Craigie had also had an interview with the Japanese Foreign Minister. Relations between this country and Japan seemed easier.*

The Japanese Foreign Minister had blatantly lied about his country's intentions in relation to Singapore, and seeing as they also bombed parts of the west coast of Australia, they weren't exactly honest about their intentions there either. Noticeably there was no mention of Japan's intentions in relation to Malaya, Hong Kong or Thailand. It was interesting to note that Sir Robert Craigie felt that relations between the two countries seemed easier.

It would appear that Japan was saying what was politically expedient to the different Allied nations, to either appease them or to keep them on their toes, while in fact she was simply biding her time, building up the collective strength of her Army, Navy and Air Force so that when she felt strong enough, and the time was right, she would strike with all her might.

# CHAPTER TWENTY SEVEN

# OPERATION ZIPPER

With the war in Europe having finished in May 1945, the planned British retaking of the Malaya peninsula from the Japanese was planned to begin on 9 September 1945. It was codenamed Operation Zipper. Thankfully, with the Japanese unconditional surrender in August 1945, the operation did not have to be implemented.

The plan was for 100,000 British and Allied troops, supported by more than 500 aircraft from the Royal Air Force, to land at and capture either Port Swettenham or Port Dickson, which are both situated half-way down the west coast of Malaya.

The operation to retake Singapore was codenamed Operation Tiderace. Amazingly it had only been planned after the Americans had dropped atomic bombs on the Japanese cities of Hiroshima and Nagasaki on 6 and 9 August 1945.

The fact that Britain did not have to go ahead with her plans to invade both Malaya and Singapore undoubtedly saved hundreds if not thousands of lives.

The landings at Penang, which is further north along the west coast of the country, went ahead as planned, but more as a means to see if Japan was adhering to the terms of her surrender. The landings met with no Japanese resistance.

When the British arrived back on Malayan soil, waiting at Penang were 26,000 troops of the Japanese Seventh Area Army who before the surrender had controlled Malaya, Java, Sumatra, Siam, parts of Borneo and part of the Nicobar and Andaman Islands. Their commanding officer was General Seishiro Itagaki, who formally surrendered to the British at a ceremony of surrender held on 22 February 1946 in the grounds of the Malaya Command Headquarters in Kuala Lumpur. This was six months after Japan had officially surrendered to the Allies.

General Itagaki had already surrendered all Japanese forces in South East Asia to Admiral Louis Mountbatten in Singapore on 12 September 1945. Operation Tiderace had actually commenced on 31 August 1945 when Mountbatten ordered Allied troops to set sail for Singapore from Trincomalee in Sri Lanka and Rangoon in Burma, but when they arrived in Keppel Harbour there was no resistance from the estimated 77,000 Japanese troops who were awaiting their arrival, and by 1800 hours the same day they had become prisoners of war of the British.

In October 1944, Tun Ibrahim Bin Ismail, a Malayan soldier commissioned into the Indian Army, was serving with the British Special Operations Executive (referred to in the Far East as Force 136). Along with two colleagues he was parachuted into Terengganu, which is situated on the Western coast of Malaya, as part of Operation Oatmeal. Unfortunately they were very quickly captured by the Japanese, but instead of being killed by the Japanese, who realized the benefits that the three men could potentially provide, they were interrogated. After a month they agreed to become double agents for the Japanese. But, having managed to inform the Special Operations Executive of their situation, they in effect became triple agents. They eventually managed to get the Japanese to believe that the impending attack on Malaya would take place in the Kra Isthmus region of the country, which was some 650 miles north of where it was actually intended.

Ismail was awarded the Order of the British Empire in November 1946. He went on to have a distinguished military career, serving in the Sultan of Johore's State Forces after the war before transferring to the Malay Regiment in 1951 and going on to become Chief of the Malaysian Defence Forces, a position he held between 1971 and 1977. He died on 23 December 1977 aged 88.

On 26 July 1945, after the war in Europe was over, the President of the United States of America, Harry S Truman, the Prime Minister of Great Britain, Winston Churchill, and Chiang Kai Shek, the Chairman of the Nationalist Government of China, met at Potsdam in Germany to discuss Japan. At the end of the conference the three nations issued what became known as the Potsdam Declaration, which in essence was a proclamation defining the terms of any future Japanese surrender.

The terms of the Declaration were:

- The elimination for all time of the authority and influence of those who have deceived and misled the people of Japan into embarking on world conquest.
- The occupation of points in Japanese territory to be designated by the Allies.
- That Japanese sovereignty shall be limited to the islands of Honshu, Hokkaido, Kyushu, Shikoku, and such minor islands as we determine, as had been announced in the Cairo Declaration in 1943.

- That the Japanese military forces, after being completely disarmed, shall be permitted to return to their homes with the opportunity to lead peaceful and productive lives.
- That we do not intend that the Japanese shall be enslaved as a race or destroyed as a nation, but stern justice shall be meted out to all war criminals, including those who have visited cruelties upon our prisoners.
- The Japanese Government shall remove all obstacles to the revival and strengthening of democratic tendencies among the Japanese people. Freedom of speech, of religion, and of thought, as well as respect for fundamental human rights shall be established.
- Japan shall be permitted to maintain such industries as will sustain her economy and permit the exaction of just reparations in kind, but not those which would enable her to rearm for war. To this end, access to, as distinguished from control of, raw materials shall be permitted. Eventual Japanese participation in world trade relations shall be permitted.
- The occupying forces of all the Allies shall be withdrawn from Japan as soon as these objectives have been accomplished and there has been established, in accordance with the freely expressed will of the Japanese people, a peacefully inclined and responsible government.
- We call upon the government of Japan to proclaim now the unconditional surrender of all Japanese armed forces, and to provide proper and adequate assurances of their good faith in such action. The alternative for Japan is prompt and utter destruction.

The conference in Potsdam had begun on 17 July 1945, the day after the Americans had carried out their first successful atomic bomb test in the deserts of New Mexico, providing them with the knowledge that the weapon definitely did work.

This was a final ultimatum on behalf of the Allies who really did not want to have to engage in a war on the Japanese mainland, as they knew that casualties, especially amongst their own military personnel, would be extremely high; so clarity on the matter was paramount.

For whatever reason, Japan didn't respond and decided to fight on, maybe in the forlorn hope and belief that the Allies were scaremongering or simply bluffing; but they weren't, which Japan was to discover with devastating consequences. The dropping of the two atomic bombs resulted in the deaths of tens of thousands of Japanese civilian and military personnel, as well as the destruction of many homes and other buildings.

It wasn't until noon on 15 August 1945 that the Japanese Emperor, Hirohito, went on national radio and announced his acceptance of the Potsdam Declaration in its entirety. The wording of the surrender document, signed on 2 September 1945 on board the USS *Missouri*, was as follows:

*We, acting by command of and in (on) behalf of the Emperor of Japan, the Japanese Government and the Japanese Imperial Headquarters, hereby accept the provisions set forth in the declaration issued by the heads of the Governments of the United States, China and Great Britain on 26 July 1945, at Potsdam, and subsequently adhered to by the Union of Soviet Socialist Republics, which four powers are hereafter referred to as the Allied Powers.*

*We hereby proclaim the unconditional surrender to the Allied Powers of the Japanese Imperial General Headquarters and of all Japanese armed forces and all armed forces under Japanese control wherever situated.*

*We hereby command all Japanese forces wherever situated and the Japanese people to cease hostilities forthwith, to preserve and save from damage all ships, aircraft, and military and civil property and to comply with all requirements which may be imposed by the Supreme Commander for the Allied Powers or by agencies of the Japanese Government of his direction.*

*We hereby command the Japanese Imperial General Headquarters to issue at once orders to the Commanders of all Japanese forces and all forces under Japanese control wherever situated to surrender unconditionally themselves and all forces under their control.*

*We hereby command all civil, military and naval officials to obey and enforce all proclamations, orders and directives deemed by the Supreme Commander for the Allied Powers to be proper to effectuate this surrender and issued by him or under his authority and we direct all such officials to remain at their posts and to continue to perform their non-combatant duties unless specifically relieved by him or under his authority.*

*We hereby undertake for the Emperor, the Japanese Government and their successors to carry out the provisions of the Potsdam Declaration in good faith, and to issue whatever orders and take whatever action may be required by the Supreme Commander for the*

*Allied Powers or by any other designated representative of the Allied Powers for the purpose of giving effect to that Declaration.*

*We hereby command the Japanese Imperial Government and the Japanese Imperial General Headquarters at once to liberate all allied prisoners of war and civilian internees now under Japanese control and to provide for their protection, care, maintenance and immediate transportation to places as directed.*

*The authority of the Emperor and the Japanese Government to rule the state shall be subject to the Supreme Commander for the Allied Powers who will take such steps as he deems proper to effectuate these terms of surrender.*

The Allies had tried their best to get the Japanese authorities to surrender and prevent any further loss of life. They had appealed directly to their government, they had carried out leaflet drops and broadcast radio messages in both Japanese and English, encouraging a surrender, but all to no avail. On the day of the second atomic bomb being dropped on Nagasaki, Japan also had to deal with the Soviet Union declaring war on her and invading Manchuria. Finally, Japan realized and accepted that her position was untenable and she capitulated to the Allies.

# CHAPTER TWENTY EIGHT

# PATRICK VAUGHAN STANLEY HEENAN

There has been much talk over the years about spies in relation to the Japanese invasion of Malaya and Singapore during the end part of 1941 and early 1942. Most of it has been no more than supposition with little or no evidence; but one man does warrant further investigation.

Patrick Vaughan Stanley was born to unmarried Ann Stanley on 29 July 1910 in the small mining town of Reefton in New Zealand's South Island. His father's details were not recorded on his birth certificate. Ann, who was 28 years of age when she gave birth to Patrick, was born in Stratford, Taranaki, in the North Island. Ann's parents, Robert and Ellen Stanley, from Liverpool in England, had emigrated to New Zealand in 1877 and settled in Stratford. Why or how Ann ended up in Reefton is unclear, but in 1910 'it looked like a Wild West frontier town, made up of wooden shacks and lodging houses straddling the main street.' A town that was home to miners digging for gold and coal does appear somewhat of an unusual choice of destination for a single woman living in New Zealand during the early 1900s.

Born some twenty-seven years before Ann in Bhagalpur, Bihar, India, in 1855, was George Charles John Heenan, the son of a civil engineer. Not too much is known about George, but in 1871 he was a live-in student at Cheltenham College in Gloucestershire. Where and when George and Ann met is not exactly clear, but meet they did and, along with young Patrick, they made their way to Burma.

In Peter Elphick and Michael Smith's 1993 book *Odd Man Out: The Story of the Singapore Traitor* it is mentioned that there was no record of Ann and George having married. This might have been because George was already married and, as a Catholic, was unable to divorce. It goes on to say that in 1912 Patrick was baptised in Rangoon. Now having acquired the surname of Heenan, his old surname of Stanley had become his second name, and Vaughan his third. His name now read, Patrick Stanley Vaughan Heenan. The plot thickens as to the possible reasons why these changes were made to his name but, just six months after Patrick had been baptised, George Heenan suddenly died. He was 57 years of age.

In 1927, Patrick, at Cheltenham College, excelled at sport, particularly athletics and boxing, although academically he wasn't the brightest. It was there that he acquired his first taste of military life when he enrolled in the college's OTC. He left Cheltenham College in 1929 and initially took an office job in the City of London where he stayed until gaining a commission as a second lieutenant in the British Army as part of the Indian Army in February 1935, although he was initially attached to the 1st Battalion, Royal Warwickshire Regiment, who were based in Poona, India. In October the following year, Patrick joined the 1st Battalion, 16th Punjab Regiment of the Indian Army, who had a long and proud history, its origins dating back to the early 1800s.

It would appear that Patrick Heenan was a man who didn't make friends that easily, and was disliked by some of his colleagues. The British Army of the 1930s was still an organisation where social class and breeding meant everything. These were two aspects of life which Patrick did not possess. The other element of army life which Patrick had to deal with was coming to terms with the fact that being an Indian Army officer meant that he was viewed by other officers of the regular British Army as being almost second class, despite being of the same rank. This was a theme that had followed him for most of his life. He continually blamed a society based on what he probably saw as an unfair and outdated class system. The reality was, I would suggest, somewhat different. In simple and direct terms, he just wasn't academically intelligent enough. In sport he certainly did have a natural prowess, but when it came to the classroom, he was found wanting. It was his inability to pass exams, both at college and in trying to obtain a commission into the Army, that stopped him from getting where he wanted in life, not society or the class system that it was based on.

When he eventually became an officer in the Indian Army, he then didn't appear to understand how to conduct himself or 'play the game'. This 'woe is me' attitude was, I suggest, his own choice. It might well have derived from the disadvantages which he had experienced in his life, and maybe to some extent from a lack of opportunities, but they were nobody else's fault but his own. The fact that he had failed to get on with so many people throughout his life, especially those in positions of authority, had not helped his cause.

Before the war in Europe had begun, which was two years before Japan's attack on Pearl Harbor and subsequent entry into the Second World War, it was not uncommon for officers of the Indian Army to take their leave in Japan. When Patrick Heenan had a period of leave, he stayed in Japan for nearly six months, engrossing himself in Japanese culture and learning to speak the language.

Although a highly probable hypothesis that Heenan was approached or 'turned' by the Japanese during this time, there is no evidence of this having actually happened.

In 1941 Heenan became part of the Indian Army Air Liaison Unit and, after completing his initial training in Singapore in June of that year, was sent to Alor Setar, which is in the state of Kedah in northern Malaya, as it was then. The British RAF had their No. 62 Squadron stationed there in the latter part of 1941, along with Squadrons from other Commonwealth nations.

Having detailed information about Allied aircraft would have proved invaluable to the Japanese and made their task of conquering Singapore much easier. Mr Sydney Tavender, who was on the same unit as Heenan, said, 'the Japanese aircraft always seemed to know the correct recognition codes, despite the fact that they were changed every 24 hours.' About Heenan he said, 'Heenan was caught during an air raid. When we discovered he wasn't in the slit trenches with us, we became suspicious, went to his quarters and discovered a radio which was still warm. That was the last we saw of him. He was arrested.' The radio set had been hidden inside an RAF chaplain's holy communion box, an object which was probably in the open for all to see every day.

By 10 December 1941, the same day that Heenan, by now a captain, was arrested, most of the Allied aircraft which had been located in northern Malaya had been destroyed by the Japanese. How much of that was down to information supplied to them by Heenan is unknown.

On his arrest, Heenan was taken to Singapore where he was reportedly court-martialled, although no actual paperwork or documentation in relation to this has survived. This could be because the Japanese destroyed the documents when they captured Singapore to hide the fact that he had been spying for them, or, equally possible, the same documents were destroyed by the British to hide the fact that they had a spy in their midst, which most certainly would not have been good for morale, either military or civilian.

The following is an extract from a wartime letter sent by Flight Lieutenant Alfred Elson-Smith of the Royal Australian Air Force to his wife. It appeared on the website ww2talk.com on 27 April 2010, posted on behalf of a man by the name of Len 'Snowy' Baynes. The letter came from Elson-Smith's book *Great was the Fall*, published in 1945, which in the main consisted of letters he had written to his wife May.

*When I reported at 7 o'clock tonight, a further shock awaited me. I have told you in past letters of a Captain Heenan who has been liaison officer for the 11th Division to the RAF stations of Alor Star, Sungei Patani and Butterworth. Well my dear here's the key to the cause of the walloping that we have had in the north up to date. Major Francis of Military Intelligence arrested him at 2 o'clock p.m. as a spy. There is no question of the authenticity of this arrest, since they got the dope which proves his guilt beyond doubt. Just realise this b- - - - - - has been living with us in our mess for four months, drinking and playing cards and joining in our general living conditions. He has had access to our operational rooms together with full and concise knowledge of our administration, in every form pertaining to our strength, possible strength and in short the guts of everything. This simplifies the whys and wherefores of this dreadful debacle and to what extent his activities have sold us out southwards, to what extent we have yet to experience. No words of mine, or anyone else for that matter, can express the feelings we have towards this man who though clever has sold us so uniquely. Of course his fate is sealed, yet the damage he has done cannot be estimated since according to his own statement when he joined us, he had completed 15 years in the army, serving in all parts of India. This man evidently controlled all the subversive elements in the northern area from the Pri River to Penang and the Thailand border and incidentally recalls to my mind the type of women he kept company with in Penang. Well, my dear, whatever I might have suspected of the natives I never gave thought to such a climax as this. No doubt the authentic information leading to his arrest will be made public one day, but you can take it from me, it was by the little things and careless indifference to our apparent stupidity that he was finally caught, and thanks to Major Francis who is certainly a credit to our military intelligence service.*

The obvious question in relation to the above letter is, how was it ever allowed to have been sent? I find it hard to believe that in a time of war a letter which spoke of such things would have ever got past the military censor.

It would appear that concerns about what Heenan might have been up to had been reported to senior military figures on more than one occasion in the years immediately before his arrest, but other than move him on to another unit, nothing substantial was ever done about him, until it was too late. By then the damage which his betrayals caused would already have been done.

He was arrested on Wednesday, 10 December 1941, near to where he was based in Malaya, and two days later, on Friday, 12 December, he arrived in Singapore. His court martial didn't begin until early in the New Year and lasted for a couple of days, at the end of which he was found guilty.

Courts martial at the time were governed by the Army Act of 1881. There are three different types of courts martial: a District Court Martial, applicable to peacetime, could impose a maximum sentence of only two years; an officer could only be tried in either a General Court Martial (in peacetime), or a Field Court Martial (in time of war). The latter court had far-reaching powers. For certain offences, such as treason, the charge for which Heenan was being tried, it could impose the death penalty. Despite the speed with which events in Singapore were unfolding at the time, Heenan was not tried in a kangaroo court hell bent on revenge; correct due process was followed.

It is rumoured that Heenan was taken down to the harbour in Singapore and shot dead. The following is taken from the wikipedia page for Patrick Stanley Vaughan Heenan. They are the words of journalist and author Lynette Silver in *Scapegoats for the Bloody Empire* (1997):

> *By February 13 Heenan had become very cocky, taunting his guards ... that he would soon be free and they would be prisoners. It appears that ... British military police took matters into their own hands. After cards were cut to decide who would kill Heenan, it is alleged he was taken to the dockside, where a sergeant executed him with a single pistol shot to the back of the head. The body was then dumped in to the harbour.*

It is hard to believe that the order to kill Heenan was taken by a sergeant of the Military Police. It must have been a decision which had been taken at a higher level and passed down to those who were charged with guarding him. Wherever exactly Heenan was killed is not absolutely clear. Even though this was war, I find it hard to believe that British military personnel would have wanted any witnesses to their actions. As this was in effect 'the eleventh hour', the harbour area in Singapore must have been a hive of activity with people trying to escape the Japanese advance. Regardless of the reasons behind what they were doing, it wouldn't have looked good executing a man in full view of other people.

Remarkably a search of the British National Archives shows absolutely no trace of anything to do with Captain Patrick Stanley Vaughan Heenan. It is as though officially he never existed.

Heenan's name still appears on both the Second World War Memorial at Kranji War Cemetery and on the Roll of Honour at Cheltenham College in Gloucester. Maybe this was part of officialdom trying to cover up the fact of Heenan's treachery. With the passing of time, a total lack of documentation having survived and many of the witnesses to these matters now dead, it is unlikely that any more information will emerge about what happened to Heenan and for how long his treachery had gone undetected.

The Commonwealth War Graves website shows the date of Heenan's death as 15 February 1944, and his parents as Mr George Charles Heenan and Mrs Anne Heenan of Cheam, Surrey. This entry is clearly incorrect. Firstly, because Heenan was killed on 14 February 1942. Secondly, because George was not his actual father; he had died on 24 October 1912. And thirdly because Patrick's mother Ann had remarried in April 1929 when she became the wife of widower Bernard Carroll with whom, along with his two young children, she set up home in Cheam. Bernard died in 1948.

# CHAPTER TWENTY NINE

# FIRST BATTALION MANCHESTER REGIMENT

The 1st Battalion Manchester Regiment had been stationed in Singapore since October 1938, and prior to that they had been in Jamaica, Egypt and Palestine starting in 1934.

They were stationed at Tanglin Barracks, which had been built for European soldiers back in 1861, but by the time the Manchesters were stationed there the barracks had thankfully been refurbished and were both modern and spacious.

There were still some two hundred officers, non-commissioned officers and men who had been with the battalion since the Manchesters had first moved abroad in 1934, and by 1942 many of them were due for discharge from the Army or to be transferred to the reserve. For them the outbreak of war couldn't have come at a worse time. But they accepted their lot, maybe with the odd moan or two, and got on with things. Many of them had not been home on leave for the entire eight years that the battalion had been away.

Many of the soldiers' wives worked either in admin, or as secretaries, or as auxiliary nurses in one of the island's many hospitals. As the threat of a Japanese invasion became more and more of a reality in December 1941, so did the speed of the evacuation of all 'unnecessary' British personnel away from Singapore. Most of the ships being used in the evacuation were heading for the safe havens of South Africa, Australia, India or England.

As the situation worsened, the Manchesters were employed in improving the island's defences. They helped build both anti-tank obstacles inland and anti-landing craft obstacles on the many beaches, but there were no obstacles they could build to stop Japanese aircraft from bombing and machine-gunning them from the skies. The first such attack came on the morning of 8 December 1941, the day after the Japanese attacked the American Fleet at Pearl Harbor. As the days and weeks went by, so the attacks increased in their intensity and the Manchesters saw their first casualties.

When Percival surrendered on 15 February 1942, the 1st Battalion Manchester Regiment were some of those who became captives of the Imperial Japanese Army, when they marched off from Singapore City to the newly designated prisoner of war camp at Changi, led by their senior officer, Lieutenant Colonel Holmes. Their new home was to be 'A' block at Selarang Barracks which before the Japanese invasion had been home to one hundred men; now it had to cater for some eight hundred men, making living conditions extremely cramped.

On 30 August 1942 the Japanese authorities surprisingly issued an order to all Allied prisoners of war instructing them to sign a non-escape agreement, which everybody refused to sign. From an Allied perspective, this was a direct contravention of the Geneva Convention on the treatment of alien combatant prisoners of war; but as Japan hadn't signed up to that convention, in their eyes they weren't actually doing anything wrong. The Japanese ultimatum came with a twenty-four-hour window of opportunity to sign, 'or else'. The 'or else' was having all prisoners of war who were being held at Changi crammed into the barracks at Selarang. Because the Allied prisoners refused to sign the agreement the threat was carried out. With thousands of men now crammed into a camp meant for just one hundred, problems were soon going to arise, with a lack of water and sanitation being top of the list. Men started to fall ill and die from dysentery and on 5 September Lieutenant Colonel Holmes instructed all of his men to sign the no-escape form, under duress. As soon as everybody had signed, matters were returned to normal and those moved into the camp from nearby Changi were moved back. Four Allied prisoners of war, Australians Breavington, Gale, Waters and Fletcher, who had managed to escape, were recaptured by the Japanese and executed by firing squad. Guards from the Indian National Army carried out the executions and so bad was their aim that the first shots did not kill the four Australians; they had to be shot again before they died.

The Japanese officer who ordered the executions, General Fukuye, was himself shot by firing squad at the self-same spot as the four Australian soldiers, after he was found guilty at the Singapore war crimes trials of 1946.

At the beginning of the Battle of Singapore on 8 February 1942, the strength of the 1st Battalion Manchester Regiment was 43 officers and 960 non-commissioned officers and men. By the time the Japanese had surrendered Singapore back to the British on 4 September 1945, and all of the prisoner of war camps had been liberated, there were 37 officers and 528 other ranks still alive. The other 438 were either killed in action during the fighting for Singapore or died in the prison camps. Private Sidney 'Buddy' Jacobs (see chapter 14) was one of those who made it home after the war.

A check on the Commonwealth War Graves Commission website shows that 57 men from the 1st Battalion Manchester Regiment are buried at the Kranji War Cemetery, another 95 are remembered on the Singapore Memorial. One man is buried at the Labuan War Cemetery in Malaysia, and another 98 are buried in cemeteries throughout Thailand, most of whom died during 1943 while working on the Burma Railway.

During the week-long battle of Singapore, the 1st Battalion Manchester Regiment lost 18 men killed in the fighting. A further 26 members of the battalion were lost at sea on the night of 13/14 February 1942 when the ship they were on, HMS *Dragonfly*, a river type gun-boat which had sailed from Keppel Harbour in Singapore on route to Batavia in Sumatra, was sunk during an attack by Japanese aircraft off the east coast of Sumatra near Rusukbuaja Island.

# CHAPTER THIRTY

# PRIVATE 5775484 MAURICE ORCHANT

Maurice Orchant was a prisoner of war in Singapore's notorious Changi Prison, becoming a captive of the Japanese with the surrender of the island which had taken place on 15 February 1942.

He had enlisted in the Army on 18 January 1940 and become Private (577548) Orchant in the 4th Battalion, the Royal Norfolk Regiment.

Maurice Orchant, who was Jewish, kept his 'treasured possessions', which in his case were photographs of his family and letters from his loving and loyal wife Fay, tucked safely away inside a book. Somewhat ironically the book in question was German. It was about mathematics and originated from the mathematics library at the Raffles College. How Maurice came to be in possession of it is unclear, but it is currently about seventy years overdue.

The first thing Maurice put in the book was a typed letter to Fay and their son Michael:

*Dearest Fay,*

*Throughout the heart breaking loneliness of this terrible separation your letters have always been my compassions, in the middle of the miseries of this POW life, they have comforted me. When I have been sad they have cheered me up. At all times I have found delight in reading and re-reading these words your loving hands have written. That is why they are …*

*"My Treasured Possessions"*

*Now such valuable letters must be cared for, so I have devoted much of my few spare hours to binding them into this book together with a few other scraps and pieces which have meant so much to me.*

*I still gaze for hours at the few and only photographs I have managed to keep all through this period.*

*I received these letters all at once, and not in the order in which they were written, and so now I have answered them and pretended that you are going to receive them.*

*Later in this book, you will find a letter, the longest letter I have ever written, addressed to you. The date and its contents you will find speak for themselves.*

*In the little pocket inside the back cover you will find the envelopes which protected your letters.*

*And so my darling I give you …*
       *"My Treasured Possessions"*
*May you get as much pleasure in reading it as I had in making it.*

*Changi*

*August 1944.*

At the time of writing, Maurice had been held in captivity for two and a half years. Malnourished and surrounded by death on a daily basis, his story is a remarkable victory of mental strength over adversity.

The book contains three photographs. One of Maurice taken sometime before the war, dressed in a civilian suit, shirt and tie. The other two, which have become badly faded with the passage of time, are of Maurice's wife Fay and their son Michael, mementoes which undoubtedly helped him get through his days in captivity.

Maurice's *Treasured Possessions* is now showing its age. But it's still alive and kicking like an old man who has seen better days but who isn't quite ready to pack it all in, just yet. The spine has come away and the front cover is separate from the rest of the book.

The first handwritten letter in the book is from Fay to Maurice and is dated 13 November 1941. According to the letter, Fay and Michael lived at 14 Gresley Estate, Ross-on-Wye, Herefordshire:

*My Dearest Husband,*

*Eventually we have arrived. I had a difficult time getting fixed with removers, we paid £10. Let me tell you just what happened. I went to the people about taking over our bit of the furniture and she came with another woman and said as her husband comes Saturday he would see everything and will leave it to him. I told her we want £7.*

*I took my material to the dressmaker and the woman hearing I was leaving Cambridge said, "why don't you let Frances," her partner, "take it, she would give you £10 for it as she must have lace." I asked Frances to come round on the Friday, before the other people. She didn't come although she said she would. On the Saturday the other people also didn't come. Monday, I went for a fitting and asked Frances why she didn't come. She said her husband had finished work late but would come after lunch. As I got home the agent came for the rent, he asked if we were moving, I said "No". He said some people had been to say that I am moving and wanted to take the place. I denied it. Dinner time Frances came over and after showing her around, I said I would take £7 as I would rather she had it. She said she would ask her husband. The next day I went in she said, "My husband would not give all that money," so I said, "We'll leave it." That night the agent banged on the door to say the girl Francis had been around and said I was going to Ross-on-Wye and he wants to know if I am leaving. I said 'No'. A week later I met a lovely Yiddish couple, he is a musician at the Dorothy Café. They are very wealthy and are willing to pay £7 if only to have the house. I went with the wife to the Landlady and said as I was moving I want to recommend a friend who was willing to give me a few pounds which it cost taking over from McDougal. She says to her, "I have a waiting list. What is your name and address," Then she asks me when I am moving, I said, "These people are willing to take over immediately, she said she also likes to see the lay of the place." So we arranged to come on the Monday at 12.20am. We had to wait an hour before she arrived, then she refused to have them. I asked this chap if there was anything I could do, then we saw the agent and he said, why not keep the book in my name and say I was letting it partly furnished. We went again to the Landlady and told her what we were going to do and she said she cannot say anything until she consults her employers. But I had fixed removers for the next morning, so this fellow said, "If I am willing to leave the few articles they would not yet move in but the wife would be in on the Monday to pay rent or if a few days go by and they hear nothing they would move in and I should trust him to send on the money. I said ok. That evening I hear a bang at the door, a mother to the neighbours at No.1, a woman saying the Landlady had given them the key as I was moving, I said that was not so. I had already let it partly furnished. I arranged for the agent to call that morning and when he did I asked if that was possible he said it was not true as only I had the key. So as I say eventually we are here and I want to see what happens. I hope you're not angry with me for writing all this down, but I want you to know everything.*

A lot of the writing on the following page is now mostly illegible, but appears to be routine information about the domestic trials and tribulations Fay is experiencing. I would imagine though, for Maurice, reading it would have been extremely interesting. The letter continued:

*You will never know how empty it felt. You away. I cuddled Michael tight all night. He gets on lovely. I ask him who is Mossy, he says, 'Daddy'. Mossy, our photos are on the sideboard in the frame and we are comfortably settled now. I have not yet given Mrs Berg anything as we have been busy.*

*I'm finishing now as Michael is stretching out his hands to me and saying "up mummy", and all send love to you. Don't let it be long before we meet again. Finish them off quickly. How are the boys?*

*Good Luck darling.*

*Fay.*

The next letter is one that Maurice has written, but I don't think it was ever actually sent. It is dated 21 August 1944, while he was still a prisoner of war in Changi and was in response to a letter Fay had written to him dated 13 November 1941. At this time the Japanese only allowed Allied PoWs to send letters or postcards back home with a maximum of twenty-five words. This letter had a lot more words than that:

*21st August 1944*

*Answering the first letter I received from you as a POW. Posted by you on Nov. 13 1941.*

*My darling wife and son Michael,*

*How pleased I was to receive your first letter to me, although it was years old. I could not rest here knowing all the work you had to do by yourself, but thank God you are settled now. On reading about the trouble you had with your neighbours, I was just dying to fly home to you and get my revenge with these people who took advantage of my absence.*

*In this letter of yours you say that you hope I am not angry with you for writing every detail to me darling, there is nothing more in the world that makes me more happier than to know exactly everything that's going on around you, so don't stop writing the way you feel that I would best enjoy.*

*Well darling by now you will know that we are not in Ireland, you can tell the woman next door that she is very lucky her husband is so near to her.*

*About myself darling, the war is over for me as I am now a prisoner of the Japanese and don't know what's in store for us, already they are taking thousands of our boys to work down Singapore to do all the cleaning up of the debris and the bodies, but thank God they haven't taken me yet, I am still cooking for the boys but not European food, 99% rice. Doctors say if they don't give us any better food we will all be suffering with vitamin deficiency, so I hope they improve the food. As you can imagine it is pretty rotten after eating mother's lovely food. Now darling I would like to tell you a little about the fighting that took place. Firstly, let me tell you that I was very lucky to be a cook all through. I wasn't doing any fighting in the front line, I was cooking for the boys. There was a time when we lost many of our men and our HQ sent back for more troops and we didn't have many to send, so they said some cooks will have to go but 'Mossy' stopped and thank God it was all over very soon after.*

*Well darling, I would write you pages of war experiences but prefer to tell you personally. Well darling, write tons of letters as I am very anxious to hear from you.*

*Well my sweet, I will close now and will write more later on.*

*Good bye and God bless you all at home.*

*Mossy xxx*

It's clear from this letter how much pleasure Maurice derives from reading about his family's routine everyday events and how much it helps him cope with his own plight. The fact that he writes letters to his wife which he knows he cannot send shows just how cathartic they are.

The second similar letter Maurice 'wrote' to Fay was in response to the letter she had written to him dated 25 June 1942:

*My darling wife,*

*I am longing to receive a letter with some photos of you and Michael inside. I should just love to see him dressed up in boots and shorts, like a little man.*

*Just imagine what a time we three will have together.*

*And now a few words about myself. I have been a prisoner for 5 months now and believe me we're beginning to feel it where food is concerned. I have been sent into town on a Jap working party, they've got me at last. Believe me darling we did work hard, food was lousy, sleeping quarters were good, but they bundled us into huts like pigs, you know darling. When I thought of our lovely bed at home with its beautiful white cushions, and the way I was sleeping on bare hardboards with a straw roof over me, no blankets, sleeping in our clothes, I could have cried.*

*We got mucked around by our 'friends' and our officers could not help us. Life is very bloody here. I hope something happens shortly as I will be forever crying if it goes on much longer.*

*When we first capitulated they said we would be home very soon, but we have been prisoners for 5 months already and still no hope of relief yet. I hope to God its over soon, what I'm afraid of is the torture for us abroad. They have taken our Chief Officers and Generals away from us and that means they can do what they like to us now. They have got rid of the heads here.*

*I wish I would have taken your advice on the station at Ross. I could punch myself when I think of it.*

*Well Fay, I will close now and write very shortly some more news. So for the present, lots of love to you Michael and family from your loving husband,*

*Mossy*

*P.S. How is my sonny boy keeping. I wish you many happy returns on your second birthday and hope to God I shall be with you on your third. Look after mummy and don't be a bad boy.*

*From your best pal. Dad.*

From 24 May 1943 all of the letters which Fay wrote were in capital letters. The first of her letters in 1944 was dated 21 January. It only contained twenty-five words, indicating that the restrictions which the Japanese had long since placed on PoWs in their control had now been imposed on their correspondents as well.

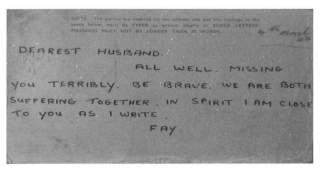

In all her correspondence to Maurice, this was the only occasion Fay had written to him in a post card.

A report from the Thailand-Burma Railway Centre, who are based at Kanchanaburi, shows that 'F' Force, which Maurice was a part of, left for Thailand on 21 April 1943 to work on the Burma Railway.

In 2009 Lieutenant Colonel Peter Winstanley OAM RFD (Retired) published an account of the horrific journey undertaken by the men of 'F' Force.

The name 'F' Force was simply a method by those in charge of the administration at Changi of keeping accurate records of all prisoners of war who were taken out of the camp by the Japanese and moved off of Singapore. The letter 'F' indicated that they were the sixth group of men that the Japanese had removed from Changi to go to work on the Burma Railway. 'F' Force was by far the largest group that the Japanese had taken from Changi. The previous five groups amounted to 7,756 men in total, 'F' Force contained 7,000. Of these 3,600 were Australians; they travelled in the first seven carriages of the train. The other 3,400 were British, and they travelled in the remaining six carriages. Some 3,200 men from 'F' Force would never return to Singapore, having fallen victim to malnutrition, maltreatment, accidents or disease, especially cholera, beriberi and malaria. Approximately 2,100 of those who died were British.

The Japanese had informed the senior British and Australian officers within the camp as early as 8 April 1943 that there was to be a large movement of prisoners out of Changi. One of the problems was that there were not 7,000 able-bodied Allied soldiers left at Changi to choose from.

The Japanese were far from honest when it came to giving the reasons for the move. They never made any mention that the men were to be used in the building of a railway. The move was supposedly to help reduce the overcrowding at Changi. They stated that food on the island was in short supply and that by moving such a large number of men out of Singapore the situation would improve and the men would receive much better food at their new destination. They also said that there would be no marching involved as trucks would be supplied for both the men and equipment, although they would have to walk a short distance from the train to their new camp when they arrived. They were to take cooking equipment, three weeks' canteen supplies, a medical party and sufficient medical supplies to last the group for three months. It all sounded too good to be true – as indeed it was.

Once those who were going to form 'F' Force had finally been selected, they underwent a series of vaccinations to protect them against cholera, smallpox, dysentery and malaria which, as it would turn out, were lifesavers for some.

The convoy of trains left Singapore on 21 April 1943. Twenty-seven men crammed into goods wagons – standing room only with only two stops per day so that the men could eat. The journey, in closed-in wagons that were made of steel, lasted for three agonising days and nights.

When the beleaguered PoWs arrived at Ban Pong, near Bangkok, there were no lorries waiting to take them and their equipment to their final destination at the Shimo Sonkurai camp, which was a journey of over 180 miles.

All equipment that couldn't be carried had to be left behind and everybody, including the 2,100 men who the Japanese knew were unfit, would have to march the entire distance to their final destination.

Maurice and the rest of 'F' Force left Ban Pong at 2230 hours on 27 April 1943 and arrived twenty days later, at 0900 hours on 17 May. The only two slightly positive notes of the journey were that the march did not start for two days after their arrival at Ban Pong, allowing the men a slight rest before they began, and the marching was done at night, out of the glare of the daytime heat.

They would spend the next eight months working on the railway. By 18 September 1943 the Australians and British had lost 1,500 men. By 9 November that number had risen to 2,200 and by the time 'F' Force had returned to Changi in early December 1943 that number had risen to 3,200.

Maurice survived the ordeal and settled back into the routine at Changi, where he would remain for another two and a half years before being repatriated back to the UK.

Amongst the letters that he kept as part of his *Treasured Possessions* Maurice had a list of twenty-five of the men he was at Changi with:

**Dick Lee** of 8 Tag Street, Bethnal Green. Dick survived the war, became a businessman and in March 1975 fulfilled a burning ambition to return to the island and visit the place that had played such a significant part in his life.

**Cyril Wernick**. According to the Commonwealth War Graves Commission website there was a lance corporal (5775444) of this name in the 4th Battalion, Royal Norfolk Regiment. He was 28 years old and died on 21 September 1945. He is buried in the Madras War Cemetery in Chennai, India. It is quite possible that he died in Madras on his way back to England after being liberated from Changi. That might explain, if it is the same man, why he is buried there.

Lew **Brody**
Ted **Venus**
Len **Goldfarb**
Dave **Gershonbeat**
Dave **Goldstein** of 6 Tomyson Street, Nottingham
Tom **Jutson**
Dick **Woodcock**
Harold **Cannon**
Bill **Clabourn** of 16 Victoria Terrace, Hornes Lane, Woolwich
Ted **Boxal** of 26 Beachfield Road, Catford, London SE6
Captain **Eaton**
Pat **Burton**
Pat **Tuhey**
Jack **Silver**
Chaim **Nussbaum**
Jack **Greenberg**
Alf **Egeliveck** of 52 Clark Street, London E1
Bert **Besser** of 26 Hope Street, London E1
Mossy **Symons**
Harry **Hughes**
**Rubens**
Jimmy **O'Connor** of 9A Fisher Street, Carlisle
Eddy **Howlett** of 66 Langham Road, London N15

During the war, Maurice's wife and son moved to Ross-on-Wye in Herefordshire. Afterwards they returned to London and had another child, a daughter named Loretta, who was born in Hackney, London. Maurice died in Poole in 2000 at the age of 82 and Fay died in 2006.

# CHAPTER THIRTY ONE

# THE DIARY OF PRIVATE CECIL JOHN SAMUEL NORRIS

Cecil John Samuel Norris, or Sammy as he was known to his friends, became a Japanese prisoner of war on 15 February 1942 with the fall of Singapore and spent the next three and a half years in captivity before he was finally liberated on 26 August 1945 from the Tamuran prisoner of war camp in Thailand. He was a private in the Royal Corps of Signals, with whom he served between 1940 and 1945.

Cecil kept a diary of his time in captivity which was an extremely dangerous thing to do. If his Japanese captors had found out, the consequences for him could have been dire.

He made notes periodically in a small booklet which he managed to keep hidden from the Japanese by either burying it in the ground or by hiding it under a pile of leaves. At the end of September 1945, while waiting in a camp at Kalyan, situated some thirty miles from Bombay, he wrote these notes up into a diary before beginning the final leg of his journey back to the UK.

Cecil never really recovered from his time as a prisoner of war, enduring poor health for the rest of his days as a direct result of his years in captivity. It was also a time of his life which he never really spoke about; he never told anybody about his diary, not even his wife Joyce whom he married in 1947. She only discovered the handwritten diary after Cecil's death in 1978 at the age of 68.

Before the Second World War, Cecil had worked in the Treasurer's Department at Billericay Urban District Council in Essex, a job he returned to after the war.

His journey began on 27 July 1941 when, along with his colleagues, he embarked on HMS *Stirling Castle*. The location of his ultimate destination at that time was unknown to him. A convoy of twelve ships would make the journey to Kuala Lumpur where it would arrive on 1 October 1941 having stopped at Freetown, Cape Town, Bombay, and Singapore on route.

The following entries are taken directly from Cecil's diary as he wrote it:

### July 29/30 1941

*Anchored there (Clyde) – nothing much happened. The accommodation on board was excellent – four in a cabin 1st class, wardrobes, washbasins, etc.*

### July 31 1941

*The convoy is underway, our destination unknown, rumoured to be Malaya.*

### August/September 1941

*A few days after leaving England I contracted severe pains in my head and chest, felt really rotten and was put into the ship's hospital. Jackie Barnes, who joined up with me in the same squads all the way, was also into hospital the same day with appendix trouble, he was operated on but died the following day. A shark was spotted following the ship some hours before he died. The funeral ceremony was most impressive. I left hospital after four days, feeling very fit. The kit of Barnes was sold by auction to us fellows, his cap badge was auctioned by progressive method which eventually reached £22 in all, nearly £100 was raised for his widow. In the mornings, Cropper and I worked in the Quarter Master's cabin writing up the ledgers. During a fog, two liners in the convoy, 'Warwick Castle' and 'Windsor Castle' collided. One was damaged so badly that it had to return to port.*

### Freetown

*After some weeks we eventually docked at Freetown where we stayed for three days. We were not allowed ashore but what we could see of the place, it didn't look as if we missed much. It was the rainy season there and it was a grand sight to see torrents of water rushing down the mountain sides, just like huge waterfalls.*

*On leaving there and subsequent days prior to our arrival at Capetown we were kept highly amused by the flying fish, sharks and dolphins. Other points of interest during this part of the journey was the scare off Dakar (supposed base for German submarines). The destroyers with us dashed off in the distance and we could see them dropping depth charges. It was rumoured that they sunk a*

U-Boat. All sorts of sports were held on deck, boxing, tennis, quoits, also a grand swimming pool. We had a very rough time in the Cape Horn and our boat tossed all over the place.

## Capetown

We eventually reached Capetown in the teeth of a gale (residents say the worst in years and much damage to beach property). What a wonderful reception the inhabitants gave us, nothing was too much trouble for them, arranging tours, dinners, dances, theatres and we went up Table Mountain, it was a grand sight. We stayed there three and a half days and none of us will ever forget the wonderful hospitality shown us.

On our way once more. The convoy split up, most of it going to the Middle East. It became obvious that we were booked for Malaya then.

## Bombay

About three weeks after leaving Cape Town we docked at Bombay and we were allowed 12 hours' shore leave. Was most disappointed for while there are many fine buildings, just behind them were the most terrible slums I have seen and the smell something awful. We rode around the town in a buggy drawn by the skeleton of a horse. Grant Road, notorious for the brothels, stripped women in cages in full view of the public. Went up Malabar Hill where we got a grand bird's eye view of Bombay. Another thing that interested me was the human scaffold, hundreds of women constructing a very lofty building, passing baskets of bricks and cement by hand around and around the building until it reached the top. We then left the remnants of the convoy in India and proceeded to Singapore on our own.

## Singapore

We made good time across the Indian Ocean and eventually reached Singapore on the 30th September amid great excitement from the troops' point of view, in the former case 'the lads' after nine weeks aboard had seen all the sea they wanted and were anxious to get on 'terra ferma' once more while for the latter it was the largest contingent of troops to land there. Much impressed by this place, and the RAF in Bristol Buffalos gave us a welcome by flying low all around the ship. Needless to say all were in great spirits when we disembarked and, thank goodness, none of us could foresee what the next four years held in store for us. On disembarking we were taken by lorries to the railway station and immediately entrained for Kuala

*Lumpur, capital of the Federal Malay States. The carriages were terrible affairs, wooden slats. We travelled throughout the night, some fellows slept on our wide luggage racks while others on the floor. After a 500 mile uncomfortable train journey in which we endeavoured to get some sleep, the smaller men are on the luggage racks while the bigger chaps are sprawled on the floor. The section I was attached to (58 strong) were all agreed that square wheels were affixed to our carriage for we were jolted about throughout the night.*

## October 1

### Kuala Lumpur

*We reached Kuala Lumpur at 6.30am the next day and while we were all dead tired we could not help admiring the beautiful Oriental buildings as we were being driven through the town in lorries to our camp, our camp at Princes Road, again a lovely white building.*

*Our home for the next two months was a large white building which in peace time was a children's school which to our delight was only half a mile from the town and once we had settled in we were quite comfortable. Allotted four to a large room, and very comfortable, as we thought, for the rest of the war, for we were all so sure that Japan would never enter the war.*

*During the months of October and November everything 'in the garden was lovely' as far as I was concerned. I had been made a 'Lance Jack' so with one stripe up I was relieved the usual fatigues we who were in the Forces know so well, spud bashing, scrubbing, guards, and the bullshit. My job in charge of petrol issues necessitated my remaining in camp alternate evenings.*

### October/November & December (5th) 1941

*I was made NCO i/c petrol. My store was a tin building away from the main buildings with barbed wire all round it. I was confined to barracks quite a lot as I was on call 24 hours a day because of convoys, 'don r's', (despatch riders) requiring petrol. However, I had a relief every other evening which enabled me to see the town and its night life.*

*Gosh, it was a great place. I enjoyed my stay there. We (Cropper, Cross and myself) became friendly with a Czech who owned a café. He was very good to us and often gave us a free meal. He fought for Germany in the last war, we were sorry to hear after we capitulated that he was killed in a car crash during an air raid.*

Cecil then went on to describe Kuala Lumpur and its people, and what they were like. He had noted that part of the city centre seemed to be made up of cafés and brothels. He described what the night life had to offer and how readily available it was. It was possible to hire a hostess to dance with for twenty-five cents; that wasn't for the entire evening, it was per dance. He commented on how petite, pretty and attractive the oriental women were and their funny little customs and quirky nuances.

### December 1 1941

### Kuala Lumpur

*Things have been looking ugly for some time and tonight we had a right 'flap,' called out at 11pm. Platts (Ration Clerk) was very drunk, so I threw open my petrol store for the lorry drivers to take as much petrol as they want while Cropper and I dished the emergency rations to the troops. Barber (my driver) and a fatigue party loaded 3,000 gallons on to my truck (Hotspot). However, at 3am we were told to stand down, allowed to lay down but not take off our equipment. From then on this became a nearly everyday occurrence.*

### December 6 1941

*Ordered to move up to war stations immediately, ours being called IPOH, 200 miles up country, ours was quite a big convoy, over 100 lorries. My truck with the mobile workshop was the last to leave, the reason for this being in case petrol being required during the journey. It was a nightmare journey, pitch black night, and the country we had to traverse was mountainous and there were no fences to prevent our going over the top.*

### December 7 1941

### IPOH

*At daybreak we pulled into the jungle for a meal and refuelling. On continuing the journey we were at a loss to understand why we received such a reception. They lined the roads and cheered wildly as we passed their village. However, we were not at a loss for long as when we reached our destination we were informed that the Nips had landed at Kota Barhu and that we were at war.*

*Johnny Gurkha was leaving the camp we had just arrived at, moving up to the front line. They certainly looked a dangerous customer and made one feel glad that they were on our side. They are grand fighters, very obedient and loyal, and they put up a wonderful show during the campaign. This camp was nothing but a sea of mud, food also very scarce. However, orders came through in the evening that the next day, we were to return, leaving just a few operating and line sections there, to Kuala Lumpur. Just like the Army!!!*

### December 8 1941

*Started on our journey back. I was allocated a spotter on the roof of 'Hotspot' also a Tommy gun for myself. Luckily we did not encounter any enemy aircraft and the only incident on our return journey was that we rode over a huge snake which was crossing the road in a wooded area. You would also laugh to see natives' faces as we dashed through their villages, no cheering this time.*

### December 9/31 1941
### Kuala Lumpur

*Life at Kuala Lumpur was a very funny one for me during this period as convoys, DRs etc, were on the move continuously. I was getting through thousands of gallons of petrol and oil daily and was therefore practically confined to barracks the whole time. Air raids became a daily occurrence. Our RAF consisted of 8 Buffalos and their first encounter with Jap fighters we lost 5 to 3 so our remaining three returned to Singapore. From then on the Japs had complete command of sky in our area.*

*Just before Christmas our sentries discovered a Jap spy dressed as a native getting through the barbed wire into my petrol dump. However he was soon interrogated and shot.*

*Under the circumstances we had quite an enjoyable Christmas. Had letters from home, Joan, Ken, Ted Berry, Aunt Marion and Mrs Germain. Dinner consisted of roast pork, potatoes, carrots and pumpkins, bread pudding and custard, chocolates, crisps and cigarettes plus one pint of beer.*

### January 12 1942
### Segamet

*Orders received to retire to Segamet 150 miles away, again a rotten journey and a sleepless one. On arrival there our quarters consisted of coolie shacks, the place was infested with snakes, rats, beetles and ants. Conditions were so bad that it was impossible to get to sleep and we sat and smoked throughout the night.*

**January 13 1942**

*A petrol dump was set up for me and a road made about 150 yards in the jungle while I was away searching the area for RASC dumps. It was amusing to see lorries coming up the mud track for a 'fill up'. Captain Harrison, the Quartermaster, commandeered a house on piles (for his blue eyed boys, Cropper and myself) on the main road. It was a two-roomed affair with a veranda around it, easy chairs, mats etc, needless to say we were the envy of the other fellows and it became a popular rest place for them. We again met Jack Cross there. He had joined a secret wireless section, which necessitated them being left behind the enemy lines operating sets. Their chances of getting away were practically nil. This was the last time he was seen and we know definitely that he was not taken prisoner so must assume that he was killed on one of those missions.*

*Another amusing incident at Segamet was that the native population used to squat around my dump all day waiting for the empty 44 gallon drums. I'll say this for them, they would not touch one until I gave permission. The first time I gave the sign for them to take them, it developed into a mad scramble and they fought each other for them, so afterwards I gave them out singly in turn. As bribes they used to bring eggs, coconuts, pineapples and bananas. The latter we could get ourselves as they were growing wild there. Sometimes we used to wander off the beaten track and sometimes find a shack in the clearing. The women of these parts were usually in their birthday suits and terrible looking specimens. Water in these parts was unobtainable, the only water we could get went for cooking purposes. It was days before we had a wash or shave, however a thunderstorm solved our problems for a while.*

**January 22 1942**

*Orders again to retire to Johore Bahru. We were machine gunned by Jap fighters as we were drawing out, luckily no casualties, although the blighters were persistent, it was hectic while it lasted. The journey to Johore was a further 170 miles back.*

**Johore**

*On our way back we passed a convoy which had been attacked by Jap fighters. Their petrol wagon was blazing furiously. The occupants had crawled under the wagon for protection from the bullets and were trapped. An officer crawled as near to the furnace as possible and shot them to put them out of their misery. We eventually arrived at our new camp, which had recently been evacuated by Aussies, under canvas. I was glad to find a ready-made petrol dump underground which I took over. As each day passed petrol became even more difficult to obtain. Dumps all over the place reserved for various services and it was a job to make them part with it. Air raids became very intensified and they came over in waves of 27, 54 and sometimes 70, their target being mainly Singapore. The British AA did some fine work and for two days we were bucked to see 12 Hurricanes in the air and they shot down a couple of Nips near us. However, the next day the Jap Air Force caught them grounded and played havoc with the aerodrome, and that was the end of our RAF. Not once did we see another plane of ours in the sky during the campaign.*

### February 1942

*The beginning of this month, it became obvious to us all that we were in a 'tight spot'. As soon as we held them in place, fresh seaborne troops would land behind our lads and cut them off.*

### Singapore Island
### Bidadary

*Orders were then given to retire across the famous causeway on to Singapore Island. Again we were under canvas at a place called Bidadary (actually spelt Bidadari and meaning 'fairy'). My petrol dump there was in the middle of a cemetery, what a cheerful sight for me, looking at a tombstone all day. It was funny to see bren gun carriers and light tanks coming through the cemetery for a refill. On the second day there, a Company Quartermaster who was left in charge of my dump in Johore, arrived and, when asked by my Quartermaster whether he had brought along this petrol I had left for the rear party, the silly 'B' replied 'No'. I was then immediately ordered to return to Johore and bring as much away as I could, and destroy the rest. I'm no hero and did not relish the job. All the time I was hoping against hope that I would be stopped by the Military Police. However, I was stopped at the Causeway and warned that if I went across it was at my own risk as they had mined it and it was likely to be blown up at any moment. However, I decided to risk it and crossed. What a desolate sight it was too.*

### Johore

*Johore normally a very busy place, was deserted with the exception of troops in ditches with anti-tank guns. Rifle and gun fire could* be heard plainly in the distance. However, I reached our old camp safely, which was deserted. The men with me had never worked so hard or so quickly in their lives. We were soon loaded and let all we could not take away with us run away. Every moment we expected the Nips to appear. However, we were soon on our way back and to our relief found the Causeway still intact. We found many dead bodies, mostly civilians lying all over the place and a charred body beside a burnt out car. The shops were well looted. However, we found one wide open so went and took a few bottles of 'pop' and some sweets. We heaved a sigh of relief as we returned over the Causeway.

Early the next morning a terrific explosion took place and the Causeway had 'had it'. As each day passed things got worse and worse, shelling and bombing throughout the day. Many a time I have dived among my petrol tanks for protection. Petrol became much more difficult to obtain. One day I was out from 8 till 4.30 before I could find a dump which was not reserved or destroyed. However, the Australian Division helped me out and gave my party a meal, cigs, and a gallon jar of rum. Another time I was referred to an amusement park which was supposed to have a dump. On walking through it I entered what used to be a large dancing hall and found the place filled with dead civilian bodies awaiting burial. There must have been hundreds of them, it was an awful sight, and I got out of the place as soon as possible, minus petrol.

The Nips made many leaflet raids, calling upon us to surrender, the leaflets were very crude. Later they called upon the Chinese and Malayan population to kiss us for rewards. On the 9th we moved to the racecourse, rumoured that 3rd corps was to evacuate the island and go to India to reform. However, that did not materialise and we received our worst 'going over' there, bombs, shells all over the place, many near misses, thank goodness. Things were most uncomfortable and on the 11th we moved to River Valley Road in to a big Chinese merchant's house. We slept in the open first night. It was marvellous lying there listening to the artillery have a ding dong with each other, it seemed that hell was let loose. We seemed to lose all personal feeling about oneself and resigned ourselves for anything.

The death rate was terrific, among the civil population mainly, and the corporation refuse carts used to collect all the dead bodies and bury them in common graves, 600 at a time. At nights the whole place was lit up, for Singapore was a mass of flames. Going through the town for petrol was a hell of a job as most of the streets were still blazing and impassable. The stench was awful as so many bodies were still buried under the debris, also people were being killed at *such a rate that it was more than the Corporation could deal with. Sewage pipes and water mains were all burst.*

*The night of the 11th was the last time I slept or closed my eyes until the fateful 15th. Every night we were on road patrol checking identity cards etc. Sniping was particularly bad, they came from all angles and many fellows were hit. One day I was in charge of a party digging a pit when an automatic opened up on us from a vacant house, did we scamper! An organised party went to investigate but the sniper had disappeared. One amusing incident against myself was that a driver wanted some black out paint for his vehicle's head-lights and the only thing I could give him was from an unopened 44 gallon drum of green paint on the tail end of my truck. He only wanted about half a pint so I tried gently easing the bung. However, the damned thing shot off and I was covered from head to foot in green paint. I looked a weird sight, so I disrobed and sat in a shallow gold fish pond in the grounds of the house and spent hours trying to get it off, it was days before it all came off.*

*Alexandra Hospital, a great disaster happened here. Japs entered the hospital and killed or badly wounded every patient, doctor, nurse or orderly they could find. They even entered the operation theatre while an operation was in progress and turned their Tommy guns on the occupants, killing them all. Orderlies and nurses were just lined up against a wall and shot. The Japs excuse for this was that firing was directed on them from the hospital buildings.*

*Food now was getting very short and there was practically no water to be had. It was a grim existence and the rumours of Nips being behind us, in front, 200 yards down the road were current throughout that time. It seemed that only a miracle could get us out of it and to be quite truthful, none of us expected to get out of it alive anyhow.*

### February 15 1942

*We have surrendered, it seemed unbelievable. Early morning we were sent to a big bridge (about 30 of us) and were told that the East Surrey Regiment were fighting a rearguard action and that they were expected to retire over this bridge. We were then to fight to a man as there was to be no retreat for us, gosh, a light tank could have wiped us out easily as we had practically no defence, just shallow trenches and the only arms we had were two Tommy guns (one I had) and the rest rifles. I don't mind admitting I really thought this was the end of poor old CJSN. I said a quiet prayer for those at home and then prepared myself for what may come. It was strange, because now I did not feel the least bit afraid.*

*Things soon warmed up for us as we were spotted by an observation balloon at the rear and soon shells came whizzing over. They struck some warehouses at the opposite side of the river about 40 yards away and a few more dropped behind us, and then all of a sudden everything went deadly quiet. It seemed so weird after all the noise during the past few days. About a quarter of an hour later all the sirens blazed the 'All Clear' signal and a messenger brought the news we had surrendered. Even now I can't explain my feelings.*

*Firstly, I was glad it was all over and that I was still alive and then later sorry that we had not fought on. Most of the night we endeavoured to help the Chinese whose junks had caught fire. When the shells hit the warehouse on the opposite bank to us, they caught fire, and as the buildings collapsed they caught the oil in the river alight. The Chinese and ourselves tried hard to get the junks away to safety but in vain, for the heat was intense. That night, after throwing our rifles, bayonets, ammo, etc. into the blazing river, we laid down and slept like logs.*

## February 16 1942

*Reported back to our camp in River Valley Road, where I tuned in on one of the sets just in time to hear Winston Churchill announce over the radio the fall of Singapore, and a very dramatic speech it was too, although we were most concerned when he stated that our death toll was very high. Although it was true, we knew how much it would worry our people at home. After the news, the Quartermaster instructed me to get an axe and bash the three £500 sets we had with us. While I was doing my stuff other fellows were picking up the bits and burying them. Later in the afternoon a party of Japs arrived and took what arms and ammo they could find and also took away our trucks.*

## February 17 1941

*Ordered to march the 18 miles to Changi, told to travel as lightly as possible, which was no hardship for me as I had had practically everything pinched (including snaps of Joan, Bid, etc.). We were allowed one lorry per 100 men, casualties etc. It was surprising as we marched through the town to find that practically every house had the rising sun flag hung from its windows. However, the lads sang lustily, calling out that we would soon be back. Decomposing bodies were lying in every road we passed through; it was a horrible sight. We arrived to find the barracks at Changi very badly bombed. However, we managed to find a building which still boasted a roof, so we settled in.*

## March April and May 1942

## Changi

*For the first fortnight, things were not at all bad, hardly ever saw a Jap and we were allowed on the sandy beach swimming all day, cricket, football matches etc. We held a test match England v Australia, the Aussie test match wicket keeper was the main thorn in our side, he scored a lovely 90 not out, which enabled them to win by 2 wickets. While the match was on, only 100 yards away the Jap fleet came up the harbour, must have been at least 40 vessels and a formidable lot they looked too. The Jap Air Force also took a delight in showing off to us, coming over in waves and flying very low.*

*Our scale of rations as laid down by the Japs for this period was: -*
*Rice 16 oz.*
*Tea 1/6 oz.*
*Ghee 1/6 oz.*
*Sugar 11/12 oz.*
*Flour 2 oz.*
*Meat 2 oz. per week.*

Although there is no mention of it in Cecil's diary, sometime during March, April and May 1942, he must have been sent up country somewhere in Malaya, because in the next section he writes about having returned to Singapore.

## May 12 1942

## Singapore

*I was sent back to Singapore on a working party, again that dreaded long march which I couldn't quite manage and got terrific blisters on my feet and finished the last two miles of the journey on the carriage in front of a Malay tradesman's bicycle. Our camo was a very dirty, smelly hole, bamboo and attup buildings which were infected with rats, lice, etc. and our job was to take hand carts into Singapore town, a distance of 2 miles, knock down blast walls and debris, fill the handcart up and take it another 3 miles to a spot where the Japs were making a big ordnance factory.*

*While in the town they did everything to humiliate us in front of the natives. Fellows were beaten up often for nothing at all. We had to make two journeys a day and I can tell you we were just about all in by the end of the day. Our pay was 10 cents a day. The Chinese were particularly good to us and used to give us food, money, cigarettes. Often when they were caught the Japs gave them a beating up. It was rotten to stand there and see someone badly beaten for trying to help you and your being powerless to prevent it. Rackets started up all over our camp. The drivers used to smuggle in tinned foods, eggs, biscuits, etc. and resold to the fellows at a handsome profit. The food was poor, rice mainly every meal. At this place I had my first taste of shark's meat, not bad either.*

*The atrocities committed against the Chinese at this period were numerous and it was quite a common sight to see 'Chinks' after having been executed, having their heads stuck up on railings. The Japs also took great delight in upsetting their roadside stalls for no reason what so ever and they used to take whatever they wanted from shops and did not attempt to pay. It did not take the natives long to realize that the Nips 'Asia for the Asiatics' was to be a one sided affair.*

*I received a couple of minor hidings, one for dropping out of the handcart convoy to buy some coconuts. It was in a way laughable, for the Nip that caught me was only about 4'6" high. I had my arms full of coconuts. He grabbed hold of one of the nuts, banged it on my head and chest, slapped my face a couple of times, kicked me on my shins and as I turned to go, planted a beauty on my behind. The other time was for taking an unofficial rest. After slapping my face a bit I was made to stand in the boiling sun holding a heavy piece of wood above my head for an hour (not as easy as it sounds). I developed an ulcer on my leg which qualified me for light camp work so Sid Barr suggested that we start a coffee racket. So we went in to business and a most successful one too.*

*We sold an average of 44 gallons per day, employed fellows to hawk it round the huts and in the first week our profit was $25.*

A check on the Commonwealth War Graves Commission website shows a Lance Corporal (2366368) Sidney Arthur Barr who died on 9 October 1943 aged 39. He was in 'N' Corps Signals, Royal Corps of Signals, and he was the same rank as Cecil.

Sidney is buried at Chungkai War Cemetery in Thailand. Chungkai was one of the base camps on the route of the notorious Burma Railway. During its construction an estimated 13,000 Allied prisoners of war died or were killed while in Japanese captivity, as well as approximately 90,000 civilians, most of whom were slave labour.

Besides being a base camp, Chungkai had its own hospital and church. Most of those buried in the cemetery were men who had died while being treated at the hospital.

Back to Cecil's dairy.

> *However, my ulcer became much worse and on 29th June 1942 I was sent to Changi Hospital where I became an outpatient. My quarters were at the NAAFI block overlooking the sea, a very pleasant spot. My leg soon healed up and I took a job in the Quartermaster's clothing store. One day, two Chinese vendors were coming across the river to sell us their wares when they were spotted by the Jap sentries who opened up on them with machine guns. Both were killed. We found one of their bodies floating the next day, so we fished it out of the river and buried him in the camp coconut grove.*

### September 1 1942

### Singapore Island

> *The Japs issued an order we had to sign a non-escape form which with the exception of nineteen men, we all refused to sign. The next day, we were then ordered to move to Selarang for punishment.*

### Selarang

> *Over 16,000 troops were herded into an area 400 by 200 yards, what a jam, we had to dig latrines right in the middle of the area, as well as cookhouses. The Japs refused to issue us with food but luckily most Battalion Quartermasters had built up an emergency reserve from previous issues so we had a little to eat, but not much I can assure you. Japs were posted all around us with machine guns, also the Sikhs who had gone over to them on capitulation, mounted guards over us. The cheerfulness of the fellows was amazing, sing songs, and they certainly had the Japs baffled. I still had a camera with me and took a roll of film of the scenes. I then smashed the camera up and later unfortunately lost the film on our subsequent trip to Thailand.*
>
> *We held out for three and a half days when diphtheria broke out, added to which the Japs had stated that they were going to bring all the wounded and sick from the Hospital into the infected area. Our senior*

*officers had a conference and decided to order the men to sign under protest to save further loss of life, they taking full responsibility for our doing so. Six men were executed there for trifling offences.*

*The form we signed was: -*

*'I, the undersigned hereby solemnly swear on my honour that I will not under any circumstances attempt to escape.'*

*The next day we were allowed to return to our former billets. However, we were only allowed to stay there for a couple of days, for we were given orders to return to the Selarang area as the Japs were bringing in large reinforcements and required our buildings to house them. We spent many days clearing up the awful mess, filling in the stupendous latrines etc. After all that I worked with the anti-malaria squad and took a course on it.*

## October 1942

*Diseases began to break out, dysentery and diphtheria being particularly bad and the hospitals were soon crowded to capacity. Deaths averaged three per day. There was great excitement when we learned that a British Red Cross ship had arrived in Singapore.*

*I was at this time living with the lads of our T M Section, a grand set of fellows. We used in the evenings to have some fine arguments which certainly helped the time to pass. However, the diphtheria epidemic hit our corner.*

*Robbo, Scobie, Young, Biggar and Moffatt all went down with it, the latter was on the SI list for some time. The remaining fourteen of us were then put in to isolation in a building well away from the main building as suspects and attended the Medical Inspection room for daily examinations.*

*Death rate increases, 17 in four days. I was detailed to attend a funeral of one of our fellows, grim affair. We have heard that the women and children internees in the jail were having a bad time of it and being badly treated, many of them died. A party of Yanks and Dutch arrived in the camp from Java. Generally, they were not in too bad shape although 12 died within the first 24 hours.*

*One amusing incident was a Yank had tattooed on his chest, below his left nipple, the word 'sour' and the right one 'sweet'. Made friends with a couple of Dutch lads, Aundry and Jon who told us that 300 of them were executed before they left Java just as a warning to the others what they could expect if they didn't behave, although thanks to the Red Cross our meals have improved. The death rate increases.*

It is noticeable while reading through Cecil's diary that he quite often swaps from imparting bad news to immediately following it up with a funny story, possibly intentionally so, to help preserve his sanity. What better way to deal with the tragic news that 300 Dutch prisoners of war had been systematically executed for no other reason than to send out a warning to others, than to follow it up with news that the meals have improved because of the Red Cross.

### November 1 1942

*Have been informed that in the near future we shall be moved to Thailand (Siam) to build a railway.*

### November 4 1942

*An advance party leaves Selarang at 9am, 40 per lorry. We were taken to Singapore station where we were packed into steel closed in goods wagons, 33 in each. It was sheer torture as one could hardly move and in all the heat of the day we were on the point of suffocation. The sides of the trucks were so hot it was impossible to touch them. For just over four days we were herded together like this, standing the whole time and it was weird to see fellows literally asleep on their feet. We were given food twice a day, one pint of rice and some dried fish, also a cup of water. However, most of us were lucky as we had still got some of our Red Cross food with us, which needless to say, helped a lot.*

*We reached Bang Pong 10am on the 8th where we disembarked and marched through the town to some bamboo huts two miles away.*

Thailand and working on the railway were to be Cecil's life for the next three years, a time in which he would see lots of his friends and colleagues regrettably fall by the wayside. He faced illness and malnutrition, which in part had left him with a 'damaged heart', an ailment that would remain with him for the rest of his life. He also suffered with beriberi, rheumatic fever, dysentery and the fear of death from allied bombing raids, but despite all of this, he survived. Because he was surrounded by death every day of his life, Cecil became almost immune to the normal feelings of humans in such circumstances, even in the case of close friends or military colleagues.

His journey from November 1942 would take him from Bang Pong, to Kanchanaburi, to Chungkai, to Wahlung, to Tamarkam, back to Chungkai, and on to Tamuran, where he was finally liberated in August 1945.

Finally, the news that all of the allied prisoners of war had been waiting to hear: the war in the Pacific and the Far East was over at last.

**August 16 1945**

**Its over ??!!!**

*The day we have been waiting for has at last arrived. None of us can realise it yet! To think that our three and a half years of misery is ended. Gosh! It's unbelievable. For the past two or three days rumours were current that the Japs were seeking terms and the Japs in camp had become even more friendlier and they told fellows that very soon they would shake hands.*

*We were having our first show in our new theatre and the programme was half way through when Ishy, the Jap commandant, sent for RSM Edkins our commander and informed him that peace was signed.*

*The first we knew of it was when Edkins and the two padres amid a crowd of fellows climbed onto the stage and announced amid deadly silence that we were 'FREE'.*

*After about five minutes of this (loud cheering) the Union Jack and the Dutch flag were hoisted and we sang 'The King' (first time allowed to sing this as Japs had banned it while prisoners), 'Star Spangled Banner' for the Yanks, then the Dutch national anthem and lastly 'Land of Hope and Glory' for the Aussies. The Padre then said a few words and we sang 'Abide with me'. After all this everyone went mad again, shaking hands with anyone, irrespective of whether you knew him or not, and although I went to bed about midnight I did not sleep a wink and I don't know anybody who did.*

**August 17 1941**

*Everyone in high spirits although a couple of incidents occurred for fellows ignoring Jap officers and they were beaten up for it. They also made us take down the Union Jack which we had hoisted up on the lookout tower last night. Needless to say, feelings are running high. The Japanese are still heavily armed and are as arrogant as ever.*

Cecil's diary continues as the buildup to the time of his actual liberation. It describes the atmosphere in the camp, his feelings about the situation he now finds himself in, as well as the general feelings of the other men as he sees them. There is understandable tension between

the men and the Japanese, who, although the war is over, are still their
captors. Men are still dying of illness, which has an ironic sadness.

The camp was visited by members of the Swiss Red Cross on August
25 1945, followed the next day by a British Paratroop officer. The day
Cecil had been waiting for had finally arrived as they prepared for the
start of their long journey back home to the UK.

### September 5 1945

*Reveille 2am, on parade 2.45am and then marched to Tamuran sta-
tion, a distance of two and a half miles. Train left there at 5am and we
made good going until we stopped at Bangbong where we were invaded
by hawkers selling eggs, pomeloes, etc. Next stop Moncompaton and
during the 20 minute stop had a quick look around the town. Quite a
nice place and a fine pagoda. From then on travelling was very slow
due to the fact that the RAF had blown most of the bridges around
this area. One huge bridge was completely destroyed. Here we had to
alight from the train and walk over a temporary bridge and for three
hours we just lounged about while the natives pushed the carriages
from our train over the temporary bridge one by one.*

### Bangkok

*We eventually reached Bangkok at 6pm and what a reception we
received there. Large crowds thronged the station and gave us a rous-
ing welcome. A reception committee had tea prepared for us at the
station, coffee, cakes, biscuits, bananas and cigarettes.*

*We were taken by ferry across the river to the main portion of the
city where lorries were awaiting us to take us to our sleeping quarters. As we passed through the streets they were lined with cheering
people and they gave us a mighty reception. We and they, cheered
ourselves hoarse.*

*What a beautiful city this is, many fine buildings, very good and wide
roads. It is called the Venice of the East, rivers run all over the place and
gondolas take people from door to door. We were billeted in huts on the
race course, the huts were converted horse stables. It was certainly the
most comfortable living accommodation we had had in years.*

### September 6 1945

*Informed that Lady Louis Mountbatten would be coming to see us
at 4pm. All on 'fatigues' cleaning camp. Later informed a party of
us (myself included) would be transferred to the aerodrome at 2pm.*

*Journey to there took over an hour as we were taken through the town on a sight-seeing tour first. Once again we received a similar reception last night. The Japs have certainly seemed to make themselves unpopular with the natives of the countries they occupied.*

*Sleeping accommodation in hangers and on 5 minute stand by notice from 7am tomorrow, destination Rangoon. Informed that deaths in Thailand amounted to over 18,000 out of 45,000 and the estimate of Tamil deaths as 150,000.*

## September 7 1945

*Boarded a twin engined Douglas Dakota at 9.30am, 25 per plane. It was a grand experience. The course flown was up the railway which cost so many lives and ran into a rainstorm which necessitated going to 13,000 feet to go above it. We found it rather cold at this height. The fellows stood up to the trip very well and only five of them suffered from sickness. The crew were a good set of fellows and handed out sweets, cigs and food. It was a queer sensation when we went into an air pocket which seemed quite often over Burma. Looking down over Burma there seemed to be hundreds of miles of paddy fields.*

*Rangoon from the air looked a massive place, but very badly knocked about by bombing. We landed at the airport at just after 1230pm, ambulances drew up to the doorway of the plane and all we had to do was step out of the plane into the ambulance (the people here apparently do not intend us to walk too far). We were then taken to a reception house where we were entertained to lunch by the first English ladies we had seen for over three and a half years. Peaches and ice cream etc. Gosh! Forgotten things like that existed.*

*From there we were conveyed to a big hospital about four miles outside the city. There we were given cigs, sweets, newspapers, had a shower and then put to bed (real beds with sheets). Given cablegrams to send home and an atrocity form to fill in. The organisation throughout has been marvellous.*

## September 8 1945

*Joan's birthday, many happy returns dear. Spent lazy day writing letters home and to Joan. Shocked to learn from newspapers of such food shortages at home, especially as there is plenty of everything here. Our meals today consisted of eggs, sausages, new potatoes, peas, meat, fruit, cream, bread, butter and jam.*

*The whole hospital staff are women, even the doctors. Vaccinated and informed that we shall move from here to India on hospital ship in about a week's time.*

## September 9 1945

*Dad's birthday, many happy returns dad. Learned with regret that one of the planes crashed yesterday on its way here, the 5 crew and 25 ex POWs were all killed. Another lazy day reading and writing to home and Joan. It's rained almost continuously, to be expected as it's still the monsoon season in these parts.*

## September 10 1945

*Lord Louis Mountbatten came to see us, stated that all Japs who had anything to do with POW camps were to be arrested and those who had committed atrocities would, as he put it, 'be strung up'. He also told us of a couple of amusing incidents. The first was that he informed the Jap C-in-Chief Burma that although the surrender terms had been signed, fighting was still continuing in some parts. The reply he got was if he would tell the Jap C-in-C where the Japanese troops were (as he evidently did not know), he would order them to cease fire.*

*The other was that the invasion of Malaya was to take place on the 8th of this month. The landings were to be at Port Dickson and Port Swettenham and the method of attack Mountbatten had ordered was a large British fleet to bombard these places for 24 hours and then send thousands of planes to destroy the defences.*

*However, as the Japs capitulated before that date this was not necessary. However, out of curiosity he landed there recently to see what the Japs defences were in the area and all they consisted of were three strands of barbed wire.*

*Another amusing incident some fellows tell me was when Lady Mountbatten visited their POW camp in Thailand. She mounted a platform, pulled up her skirt and said, 'Have a good look boys, as I know it's years since you have seen a pair of lady's legs,' and on inspection she came across a fellow wearing his 'G-string'. When he bolted for cover, she laughingly remarked that she had often heard of our clothing for the past years and was glad to have a chance of seeing what we wore.*

### September 11 1945

*Read most of morning. In the afternoon visited Rangoon, saw the famous gold pagoda. The town itself very badly damaged as it had been continuously under bombardment since 1942. The water mains and sewers badly damaged and most of the town flooded by the broken mains. It was laughable to see the Burmese washing themselves and clothes in the streets.*

### September 18 1945

*Start yet another stage of our journey home. Awakened at 5.30am and told to be ready for 6.30am. Removed by ambulance to the docks in Rangoon. Embarked on the hospital ship 'Dorchester', 9,000 tons. Five hundred of us on board and the accommodation was 1st class and had every comfort. Lunch consisted of soup, meat, carrots, potatoes, fruit and custard. For the first time in years we ate off china plates and drank from cups. Surprising how much nicer everything tastes eating off of them. At 3pm we weighed anchor and got under way, destination Calcutta. On deck most of evening, beautiful moon up and slight sea swell.*

### September 21 1945

*On disembarking, ladies of the Red Cross thrust packets of sweets, biscuits, cigarettes, matches, etc. upon us as we were getting into the ambulances. We then proceeded through the town to the transit camp which reminded one of a holiday camp. White ground floor buildings, large lawns in front etc. Here we were again medically examined. Those who the Medical Officer did not consider fit would go to a hill station at Ranchi while the fit would continue their journey home in a few days. Luckily I came in to the latter category.*

### September 24 1945

*Moved to Viceroy's house at Belvedere; it's a huge and beautiful building, large grounds, swimming and boating pools. Tables for four in the dining room, waiters, and the food was excellent. Most of the day was spent going from one office to another giving information at each. At the QM stores we were given more kit including overcoat, battledress, etc. The remainder of the day we spent in the quiz room which contained books and papers of happenings at home and abroad during the past four years, also tons of photographs of conditions everywhere. It was most interesting and we spent a good part of our time in this room during our stay, bringing our knowledge up to date.*

The next day Cecil and his colleagues received 'Movement Orders' informing them that they were on the move again the following day. This time they were going to a town called Kalyan, which was near the Indian city of Bombay.

### September 26 1945

*As train was due to leave for Kalyan at 15.35, spent most of morning taking it easy in the Quiz room. After a spanking lunch we (eight of us) were taken to the station, where we were met by lady Red Cross officials who conducted us to our carriages, four to a carriage and a sleeper each, nice beds and our own bathroom and lavatory. They gave us tea and biscuits and generally made a fuss of us. One amusing incident happened just before the train pulled out. An officer attempted to get into our carriage but was stopped by the chief lady Red Cross official who told him that this carriage was reserved 'for the people who matter'. Gosh, what's the Army coming to?*

### September 28 1945

### Kalyan

*Arrive at Kalyan at 10pm. The journey across India took 43 hours. This place is approximately 30 miles from Bombay. Lorries met us at the station and brought us back to camp. It is hilly country and nicely situated. Sleeping quarters in bricked huts. Issued with yet more kit, now have two kit bags practically full. Still troubled with prickly heat, otherwise ok. We are well away from the village and we have to make our own amusements, play darts, table tennis etc. in the canteen, and the lorries are at our disposal if we wish to go to the cinema.*

### October 5 1945

*Left Kalyan at mid-day. After much waiting about in the usual Army style, we arrived in Bombay about 4pm, conveyed by lorry to docks, were given tea and biscuits by Red Cross officials while waiting for 'repats' to board the ship, HMS Orion. We eventually got aboard at 5.30pm, but the ship didn't sail until 9am the following day.*

It was quite a relaxing journey home for Cecil and everybody else on board the ship, if a slightly overcrowded one, but after what most of them had been through over the previous three and a half years, this paled in to insignificance – they were going home. Their journey took them through the Arabian Sea, and the Red Sea, where Cecil saw dolphins and whales.

They continued their journey, passing through the Suez Canal on 14 October, and stopped at Port Said in Egypt the following day for 12 hours, mainly for refuelling. Onwards they went, getting closer to home, passing North Africa and Gibraltar, where they stopped for two hours to collect mail destined for the UK, before carrying on through the Mediterranean. Up to now the entire journey had been blue skies and calm seas. The Bay of Biscay changed all of that, where the seas became rough and the skies were no longer blue.

Cecil arrived back in the UK on 21 October 1945 after a long journey, one that many of his friends and colleagues weren't so fortunate as to have been able to make.

Reading through Cecil's diary was a pleasure and an honour, and once I started reading it, I simply couldn't put it down. The pain and suffering he endured at the hands of the Japanese along with his friends and colleagues was a vivid history of his three and a half years in captivity. The propensity for barbaric wanton violence, neglect and suffering that the Japanese seemed to enjoy inflicting on those who came under their control was only matched by Cecil's steely determination to stand up to it and make sure that he survived. The constant flow of humorous anecdotes included in his story lightens his experience, but without any disrespect to the memories of his brave colleagues and friends who didn't survive.

## Conclusion

It is for you, the reader, to decide where you think the blame lies for the capitulation and surrender of Singapore, but I will still provide my insight.

There were undoubtedly mistakes made by senior British military officers before and during the Battle of Singapore which did not help matters. Why Percival decided against building any defences along the island's northern shores is anybody's guess. All he could come up with by way of an explanation was that such defences made a negative impression on his troops. Putting in place such defences, especially when he had sufficient engineers with him to carry out the works, could have prevented the Japanese from making their way on to Singapore quite so easily, or altogether. That could have meant fewer deaths, both military and civilian; it could have prevented more than 80,000 Commonwealth troops spending more than three years in squalid Japanese prisoner of war camps where they were maltreated, brutalised, died of disease or were murdered; it could also have saved the deaths of thousands of Chinese civilians in the Sook Ching massacres.

Even when senior British military personnel were aware that the Japanese had landed in Singapore and had already gained a foothold, they decided not to move much-needed food and ammunition dumps, instead allowing them to fall in to the hands of the Japanese; this was unforgiveable.

Why Percival decided to surrender to the Japanese without knowing the size of their army, or without initiating a counter-attack is also not clear. Percival was a highly-decorated, brave and aggressive officer, who could have been expected to defend his position under almost any circumstances; but, for whatever reason, in Singapore in early 1942, he surrendered. One can only assume that he knew how many able-bodied men he had under his control and that he believed they were too greatly outnumbered.

There was also a degree of arrogance on the part of the British, which came back to haunt them with a vengeance. There was a strongly held belief amongst senior British Army officers that Japanese soldiers were inferior when compared with Commonwealth troops.

Having said all of that, I believe that Britain began losing Singapore in the years between the First and Second World Wars. There was too much indecisiveness, coupled with a mentality that the Far East wasn't a priority. Britain's priority was undoubtedly the war in Europe and there was a belief that there was no way Japan would become embroiled in a war with both Britain and America at the same time.

Tanks that would have made a big difference in Malaya were inexcusably moved to help in Russia while two squadrons of Blenheim medium bombers were moved from Singapore to India.

Some of the Allied troops who turned up in Singapore in late 1941 were unprepared, had no fighting experience and were thrown in at the deep end.

Winston Churchill, who had described the surrender of Singapore as the worst moment in British military history, refused to allow an enquiry into what happened, claiming that there was not enough time or the personnel to undertake such an enquiry while there was still a war in Europe to be fought and won. What was even more surprising was that there was no enquiry carried out after the war by subsequent British Governments. It begs the question, why?

One thing is for certain, if the Americans hadn't dropped the bombs on Hiroshima and Nagasaki, the Japanese would not have surrendered and thousands more Allied military personnel would have been killed in their attempts at freeing all of the nations who had fallen under Japanese rule; thousands more civilians would have died, and there would have been countless more Japanese atrocities as Japan's position became more and more untenable.

## References/Sources

British National Newspaper archive
Commonwealth War Graves Commission
National Archives
ancestry.co.uk
colonialfilm.org.uk
fepow-community.org.uk
historylearningsite.co.uk
naa.gov.uk
navy.gov.au
straitstimes.com
ttc.edu.sg
ukwarcabinet.org
wikipedia.com
wrecksite.eu
1942malaya.blogspot.co.uk
*"Scapegoats for the Bloody Empire" (1997) Edward Docker & Lynette Silver.*
*"World War Two" (Magazine) Orbis Publishing.*
*"Great was the Fall" (1945) A D Elson-Smith.*
Singapore History, Consultants at Battlebox.

# INDEX